J.F. PENN
PILGRIMAGE

Lessons learned
from solo walking
three ancient ways

Pilgrimage: Lessons Learned from
Solo Walking Three Ancient Ways

Copyright © Joanna Penn (2022)

All rights reserved. No part of this publication may be reproduced, stored in a retrieval system, or transmitted, in any form or by any means, without the prior written permission of the publisher.

Paperback ISBN: 978-1-915425-17-1
Special Edition Paperback ISBN: 978-1-915425-18-8
Large Print ISBN: 978-1-915425-21-8
Special Edition Hardback ISBN: 978-1-915425-19-5
Ebook ISBN: 978-1-915425-16-4
Audiobook ISBN: 978-1-915425-20-1
Workbook ISBN: 978-1-915425-22-5

Published by Curl Up Press

Requests to publish excerpts from this book, or media enquiries, should be sent to: joanna@JFPenn.com

Cover and interior photos: Copyright © Joanna Penn (2022)

Scallop shell motif created by Joanna Penn on Midjourney

Cover and Interior Design: JD Smith

www.CurlUpPress.com

For Jonathan. Always.

CONTENTS

Preface 1
Introduction 7
Why pilgrimage? 12
A personal faith 19

Part 1: Preparation — 29

   1.1 Which pilgrimage? 31
   1.2 Walking alone or with others 39
   1.3 Planning the route, maps, and navigation 49
   1.4 Physical preparation and training 63
   1.5 What to take with you —
        and what to leave behind 69
   1.6 Preparing for the inner journey 79
   1.7 Facing fears 85
   1.8 The day before: Southwark, London ... 97

Part 2: The journey — 105

   2.1 The pilgrim's day — 107

   2.2 Walking in the path of history puts life in perspective — 111

   2.3 A glimpse of the divine in sacred places — 123

   2.4 Hardship as an element of pilgrimage — 135

   2.5 Embrace the pilgrimage industry — 149

   2.6 Eating on pilgrimage — 157

   2.7 Facing the challenge — 163

   2.8 Pilgrimage in a changing season — 171

Part 3: Arriving and the return — 179

   3.1 Arriving on a pilgrimage — 181

   3.2 Returning home — 189

Conclusion: The end is the beginning — 199

Epilogue — 203

Enjoyed Pilgrimage? — 205

About J.F. Penn — 207

Books by J.F. Penn / Joanna Penn — 209

Appendices, workbook, and other resources — 213

Appendix 1: Questions by chapter — 215

Appendix 2: Practicalities of the Pilgrims' Way 225

Appendix 3: Practicalities of the
St Cuthbert's Way 231

Appendix 4: Practicalities of the Camino
de Santiago Portuguese Route 237

Appendix 5: Gear and kit list 243

Appendix 6: Selected bibliography 251

Acknowledgements 255

PREFACE

> "In the middle of the journey of our life
> I came to myself within a dark wood where
> the straight way was lost."
>
> —Dante Alighieri, *The Divine Comedy*

Pilgrimage attracts the seekers. Those with a question to answer, a problem to solve, a sin to atone for, an illness to be cured, a prayer to be answered. Pilgrims walk with a desire to make a change, to mark a boundary from one life to another, to heal, to escape.

I needed all of these, and more.

Perhaps you do, too.

PILGRIMAGE

In mid-October 2020, I walked the Pilgrims' Way from Southwark Cathedral in London to Canterbury Cathedral in Kent, England.

The following year, in October 2021, as I recovered from COVID-19, I walked the St Cuthbert's Way from Melrose in Scotland to Lindisfarne, Holy Island, on the north-east coast of England.

In September 2022, I walked the Camino de Santiago along the coastal route from Porto, Portugal to Santiago de Compostela, Spain.

These three solo pilgrimages helped me through a 'dark wood' in my life and changed how I see the way ahead.

In this book, I share my lessons learned and insights from walking these ancient ways, as well as historical, religious and cultural aspects, and plenty of tips. There are also questions for you to consider around your own journey.

Part 1 goes into practical and spiritual preparation before pilgrimage, including how to make decisions about the route and whether to walk solo, as well as what to take with you, and how to face the fears that might hold you back.

Part 2 covers the journey itself with the practicalities of the pilgrim's day, as well as how walking the path of history and facing the challenge of the way can give you much-needed perspective on life — and perhaps even a glimpse of the divine.

Part 3 addresses the arrival at your destination, and how to leave room for the gifts of pilgrimage to emerge after your return home, as well as how my three walks impacted my experience of mid-life.

At the end, you'll find appendices with practical tips for each of the three ways, as well as a gear list and bibliography for further reading.

I hope you find this book useful if you feel a call to pilgrimage, or a need for change in your life. These three walks have certainly been pivotal for me.

You can find a version of the appendices, with links to more resources and downloadable extras, at: www.jfpenn.com/pilgrimagedownload

There is also a Companion Workbook with all the questions from the book which you can download as a PDF edition or buy in print at: www.jfpenn.com/pilgrimageworkbook

"IN THE MOMENT OF DARKNESS, *the call comes.*"

PHIL COUSINEAU

INTRODUCTION

"There is an unrest in my gut that feels like hunger... I have learned to walk at these moments. I have learned to walk until the heat goes out of it."

Katherine May, *Wintering:
The Power of Rest and Retreat in Difficult Times*

It was an early autumn morning, and a chill wind blew along the river Avon. Dead leaves in shades of rust spun from bare branches and spiralled into the rushing waters below. The river was swollen and high from heavy rain, running muddy and brown, thick with sediment and debris. Larger logs, toppled by the storm, drifted in the current. The air had a scent of smoke from a bonfire at a local urban farm, a pyre for what was no longer needed.

I stood on the footbridge over the river and looked down into the depths, thinking of how

PILGRIMAGE

Virginia Woolf had filled her pockets with stones and walked into a river just like this.

How easy it would be to do the same.

It was September 2020, and I was not okay.

But then, who was at that time?

The World Health Organisation had announced the COVID-19 pandemic on my forty-fifth birthday in March 2020 and the world was mostly locked down, confined, sheltering in place.

I was lucky to have a home and an income and a loving husband, Jonathan. All I had to do was obey the rules and stay safe while the virus ran its course. I had no right to feel this way.

In those early months, countries closed their borders, and the media was filled with terrifying stories of rising deaths and debilitating sickness. There was madness in the air, fuelled by the incessant news cycle and social media contagion.

That summer, England had some glorious weather, and many people talked about being grateful for the pause the pandemic provided, for more time with their families, for the change to working from home. It was a vain attempt to reframe a situation that was unsustainable for such social creatures.

Yet sustain it, we did.

Everything was shut. Schools, restaurants, offices, cafes and shops. There was even yellow hazard tape over the playground in the park. It was quiet, except in the supermarkets, where there was a barely controlled sense of panic. There were stickers and markers on the floor, so people stayed two metres apart, and constant reminders to wear a mask and use sanitiser. People weaved around each other on paths, avoiding even the most basic human contact.

I was angry at myself for taking the freedoms of life for granted, for assuming that everything would stay the same, for working on things that didn't really matter in the grand scheme of things.

But as the months passed, and we walked the same paths near our home over and over, I wore a groove in my life. It grew deeper every day and became harder and harder to climb out of.

Life was comfortable and safe if we just stayed at home. So many people were worse off than me. I didn't have any right to be angry or depressed — and yet, I couldn't seem to escape the misery.

In the time before, I would never stay still for this long. I would always have another trip planned, another place to visit, another itinerary to be excited about. The pandemic destroyed the joy of travel, although of course, that is the least of what it has stolen.

As the months of restrictions continued, my wanderlust shifted into *fernweh*, a German word meaning 'a longing for far-off places.' The time of enforced stillness intensified it so much that, at times, it spilled over into frustration and anger — at the world, at the virus, at myself — for not being able to quiet the need to get away.

Much of the time, I maintained an outwardly positive attitude, but inside, I was a ball of rage. Jonathan said I seemed sad all the time.

I'd been struggling with insomnia for almost a year by then, waking just after two a.m. every morning and often not sleeping again. I began doom-scrolling on my phone, incessantly following the latest news and opinions on Twitter as the death toll grew. I knew it wasn't helping, but it became a compulsion, a connection to the millions of people round the world going through the same thing.

We were collectively experiencing the stages of grief around the pandemic: denial, anger, bargaining, depression — and perhaps, one day, acceptance. I was a caged bird bashing my wings against the bars, desperate to get out and back to freedom. I had to do something before I damaged myself beyond repair.

I could not control the pandemic, but I could walk out the door with my backpack. I could take one step at a time all the way to Canterbury Cathedral. Perhaps I could walk my rage and grief into submission and find a new path for myself in mid-life.

Resources:

- WHO announces the pandemic, March 2020 — www.who.int/director-general/speeches/detail/who-director-general-s-opening-remarks-at-the-media-briefing-on-covid-19---11-march-2020
- That discomfort you're feeling is grief by Scott Berinato, Harvard Business Review, March 2020 — hbr.org/2020/03/that-discomfort-youre-feeling-is-grief
- *On Grief and Grieving: Finding the Meaning of Grief Through the Five Stages of Loss* — Elisabeth Kübler-Ross and David Kessler
- *Finding Meaning: The Sixth Stage of Grief* — David Kessler
- *Wintering: The Power of Rest and Retreat in Difficult Times* — Katherine May

WHY PILGRIMAGE?

"*Solvitur ambulando.* It is solved by walking."
—Saint Augustine

Historically, pilgrimage has been defined as a journey to a sacred place, taken for a religious reason. But perhaps it needs to be redefined for our increasingly secular age. Many of today's pilgrims seek meaning from their journey but don't adhere to a particular religious tradition.

Pilgrimage is a physical journey to a particular place, but it's also an exploration of what it means to be human in a temporal body. Walking day after day breaks down the outer layers of the modern world through hardship in the elements. It reduces each day to walking, eating, sleeping — the basic acts of a human life. We are part animal, part spirit, and pilgrimage engages both sides.

It's also a linear journey with a beginning and an

end and a way to get from one to the other. Life itself is never so straight-forward and clear-cut, so pilgrimage provides structure and boundaries for periods when life feels storm-tossed.

There is always hardship, but the pilgrim determines the shape of the challenge by their choices of where to sleep, what to carry, who to go with, and how much preparation to do. The way will provide surprises and the pilgrim will have to adapt, but the resilience gained can pay huge dividends for the rest of life.

The call to pilgrimage

> "In the moment of darkness, the call comes."
> —Phil Cousineau, *The Art of Pilgrimage*

I first heard about the Camino de Santiago in my late teens. *The Pilgrimage* by Paulo Coelho made its way into my hands and sparked something in my imagination that would rear up many times over the following years. Whenever life challenged me, I wrote in my journal that I would walk the Camino some day, in the hope of a transformation.

I still have all my journals and I find mention of pilgrimage sporadically over the years. When I burned out in London at the Millennium and left England for Australia. When my first husband left me and I struggled through divorce. When I hated my corporate job so much, I cried in the bathroom most days, trying to find a way to escape those golden handcuffs.

Each time, I resisted the call to pilgrimage and found solace in other travels: The desert of Western Australia and the shores of New Zealand, the ancient places of Egypt, and eventually, back to London for a new life as an author entrepreneur.

But the Camino kept calling.

It is a mythical pilgrimage, the idea of it perhaps more powerful than its reality, compounded by the romanticised books of countless writers since Coelho.

When the pandemic hit and the world locked down, my desire to walk the Camino rose once more. But by then the virus raged, and it was impossible to travel. I had taken for granted the fact that I could walk it anytime, putting off the decision for decades, and now the opportunity might be lost forever.

Since I couldn't travel far, I researched pilgrimages in England and decided to walk the Pilgrims' Way, a medieval route from London to Canterbury made famous by Chaucer's *The Canterbury Tales*. It would be my first solo multi-day walk and my first step towards walking the full Camino.

There is never a right time to go on a pilgrimage, but if you feel the call, then heed it. You never know when it might become impossible for you.

If you've lost direction in life, pilgrimage can help

A pilgrimage is a specific task with a clear direction.

You have a starting point and a destination and, if you follow the way-markers, you have a route to get there.

Once you are on the trail, whichever that might be, the pilgrim's day is much the same — pack up, walk, eat, rest, sleep. You might get lost for a short time, but if you keep going, you will reach the end.

A pilgrimage journey may be the clearest path you will ever follow in life, with only a few basic choices to make each day. That minimalism can be a great comfort in difficult times.

You have no purpose but to get up and walk, and if you make it to your destination for the night, you have achieved your goal. The daily difficulties of normal life fade away as you deal with the immediate issues of pain and hunger and exhaustion. You sleep satisfied, and tomorrow you get up and do it again.

Pilgrimage brings perspective

Walking every day shrinks life down to its basic elements. You appreciate the simple things — shelter from the rain and wind, a hot shower after a long day, painkillers and blister plasters, coffee in the morning or a cold beer when the sun is high, local bread and olive oil when you're hungry, an encouraging smile from another pilgrim.

Once you step away from your normality and see how other people live, once you experience being uncomfortable, or in pain, somewhere you can't control your environment, you will be grateful for what you have and what you will return to. It's too easy to take these comforts for granted until they are lost, even temporarily.

I travel partly because it helps me see how insignificant I am on the face of the world, and walking intensifies this feeling as it is so slow. When I look at a map at the end of the day, I have only crossed a tiny part of a tiny area in a little corner of the world. I can only move at my pace, which for me is what English walkers call 'bimbling,' a relaxed gait, stopping regularly for photos, taking notes, or coffee when available.

When at home, the daily grind of life makes everything feel important and urgent, and I have to operate at an ever-faster pace to get everything done. It's easy to get stressed about a deadline or the emails that pile up, or the jobs that always need doing. Perspective narrows, even as we worry about the bigger things we can't control — the economy, war, disease.

But when on pilgrimage, I am just another human walking on the face of the world, a tiny speck in the grand scheme of things, a flash of light gone so quickly. The waves of the Atlantic will continue to crash on the shores of Portugal after my Camino footsteps have washed away. The Cathedral of Santiago de Compostela will welcome more pilgrims after I have gone. The same words of the Mass will be spoken by the next generation. I am comforted by my insignificance, and I return from pilgrimage with a new perspective on what is truly important.

> "Every day I walk myself into a state of well-being and walk away from every illness; I have walked myself into my best thoughts, and I know of no thought so burdensome that one cannot walk away from it."
>
> —Søren Kierkegaard

Questions:

- Why are you interested in pilgrimage rather than another kind of journey?
- What might pilgrimage give you? Why do you need that?
- Do you feel called to a particular pilgrimage? Why is that?

Resources:

- *The Art of Pilgrimage: The Seeker's Guide to Making Travel Sacred* — Phil Cousineau

A PERSONAL FAITH

You don't have to believe in a specific religion to want to walk a pilgrimage, but perhaps there is something within each pilgrim that is drawn to the spiritual. A sense of wanting to see beyond the veil.

Your experience of God — whatever that means to you — will be different to mine and will shape your pilgrimage. I respect your journey and I hope you will respect mine.

In this chapter, I talk about how I found God and lost Him again, and what remains of my faith.

I found God when I was fifteen.

I stood amongst a crowd of evangelical believers in a chapel in Bristol, England, hands raised to heaven, as we sang along with a band. As the last notes of the guitar resonated in the chapel, those around me spoke in tongues and called the Holy Spirit down among us. I felt a welling up inside, a desire to be part of this loving community.

Whether it was God calling me — or mass hysteria — I became a Christian that night. I went to the altar and knelt for a blessing, and was accepted into the community as a believer. I felt like I had come home.

Over the next few years, I became a leader in the local church youth group and traveled to Berlin for Love Europe, a Christian mission, one summer. I took a year out before university and worked in Exeter in the south-west of England for a Christian charity, helping to spread the word about Jesus in schools and on camps for young people.

I also traveled to Palestine several times, helping in schools and charities and working for peace. Those trips fuelled my desire to study Arabic with a goal to join the foreign office or the United Nations. I firmly believed that peace was possible in the Middle East and I wanted to be part of making it happen.

I started a degree in Arabic at the University of Oxford, Mansfield College, in the autumn of 1994. Within the first few weeks, it became clear the degree was not a good fit, and I asked my tutor what I could do to stay at the college. I'd already taken a year out and my mum had moved to the USA, so I had nowhere to go home to. Besides, I wanted to stay at Oxford. I loved my college, I just couldn't manage the language degree. Since I already knew Ancient Greek from previous studies and had a good knowledge of the Bible, I wrote an essay on Gnosticism which resulted in my acceptance into the Theology faculty.

But as I wrote essays about the historical Jesus and the Early Church, as I translated the New Testament from Ancient Greek, as I studied Israel before and after the exile, my evangelical faith ebbed away. So much of what my church had taught me was based on emotion, not truth.

When I went back to church in the holidays, all I could hear was the pastor twisting Bible verses to suit a way of life I was beginning to question.

That year, 1994, the serial killer Jeffrey Dahmer became an Evangelical Christian and was baptised in prison. My pastor said Dahmer would now go to Heaven, that God forgave his sins as He would forgive any who truly repent.

In the same sermon, he said that sex before marriage was a sin.

I could not equate Dahmer's serial murders, necrophilia, and cannibalism with wanting to make love with my boyfriend. Yes, I was nineteen, and I *really* wanted to have sex! — but I also didn't want to be part of a church that couldn't see evil for what it was.

Of course, I know that 'religion' is not God.

I know that a specific pastor or specific church does not represent faith as a whole.

I know, love, and respect many people of different faiths.

But I am not a Christian. I do not believe that Jesus is the Son of God and died for my sins. Yet the heart of a seeker remains inside me.

I have experienced the divine in sites of great natural beauty, and in places where the veil is thin and seems out of time, resonant with the faith of those long past.

I will light a candle in a church and whisper a prayer to keep my family safe. I will leave a stone on a grave. I have poured out water in the desert as an offering to the spirit of the land.

Even while my evangelical faith waned and I left the church, I remained fascinated with religion. I specialised in the psychology of religion at Oxford and I wrote my thesis on obedience to authority figures. Stanley Milgram's electric shock experiments proved that most people will do unacceptable things when 'following orders.' If the ultimate authority figure is God, then, of course, humans will do unacceptable things in His name.

Why did Abraham take his only son, Isaac, to the top of Mount Moriah, bind him to an altar, and draw the knife for sacrifice? (Genesis 22:2)

Why did Christopher Scarver murder Jeffrey Dahmer in prison in 1994?

Why did Yigal Amir, a right-wing extremist Jew, assassinate Israeli Prime Minister, Yitzhak Rabin in 1995, dashing hopes for peace in the Middle East for a generation?

They all said that God told them to do it.

After Oxford, I went into consulting and spent thirteen years implementing SAP financial software in corporations across the UK and Europe, then New Zealand and Australia. Eventually, my fascination with religion re-emerged in my fiction.

My ARKANE thrillers are based around a British secret agency solving religious mysteries around the world, in the vein of *The Da Vinci Code* by Dan Brown. My main character, Morgan Sierra, is my alter ego and her musings on faith and religion often reflect my own. My research into obedience to authority even underpins the plot for *Crypt of Bone, ARKANE #2*.

I've also written about places I later visited on pilgrimage. The Cathedral of Santiago de Compostela features in a pivotal scene in *Stone of Fire*; Lindisfarne, Holy Island, is in *Day of the Vikings*;

and Canterbury Cathedral is a setting in *Tomb of Relics*. All my stories have an element of the supernatural because the question of what lies beyond this physical realm still fascinates me.

I don't believe in a personal deity who cares about each individual and watches over my daily life, and I don't believe in a life after this one.

I believe this physical body is all I have, and after I die, everything I am is gone. Perhaps the desire to leave something behind is part of why I write. Of course, this is hubris, for every generation is forgotten all too soon.

But in the depths of pandemic misery and mid-life ennui, pilgrimage called me once more. Perhaps it was the desire to find answers and healing, the realisation of the brief span of life, or the proximity of the grave. I certainly glimpsed the divine while walking alone in nature and in the glorious cathedrals that stand as testaments to faith. I may have lost my religion, but I am still a seeker. I am still a pilgrim.

Questions:

- Is pilgrimage a matter of faith for you?
- If yes, how can you incorporate your belief into your preparations in order to make the pilgrimage even better?
- If no, are there ways you can open yourself up to the possibility of spiritual moments along the way?

Resources:

- *Murder in the Name of God: The Plot to Kill Yitzhak Rabin* — Michael Karpin and Ina Friedman
- *Obedience to Authority: An Experimental View* — Stanley Milgram and Philip Zimbardo
- ARKANE Thrillers by J.F. Penn — www.jfpenn.com/fiction and available in all formats on all online stores, or request in your library/local bookstore.

"SOLVITUR AMBULANDO, *It is solved by walking.*"

ST AUGUSTINE

PART 1: PREPARATION

1.1 WHICH PILGRIMAGE?

Pilgrimages vary in terms of distance and terrain. Some routes are well-marked, while others require navigation skills. The kinds of facilities and support available along the route will vary as well. Your choice about which pilgrimage to take can determine how easy or hard your journey will be.

Country and area

There are pilgrimages all over the world to places of spiritual meaning for different faiths, so the first decision is whether to walk nearer your home or travel further away. My Western European Christian cultural background and the fact I live in England shaped my pilgrimages. Your choices will be influenced by where you live and your cultural and religious upbringing and beliefs.

I walked the Pilgrims' Way to Canterbury in a gap

of time between lockdowns, and I'm grateful that the pandemic forced me to stay in my own country. If I could have traveled abroad, I would have, and subsequently missed out on a journey that was an important stepping stone towards my Camino.

I decided to do the St Cuthbert's Way the following year as overseas travel was still restricted and it turned out to be one of the most beautiful and memorable walks I have ever done. Walking across the tidal sands to Lindisfarne and staying on Holy Island after the crowds had gone, watching the dawn over the sea, are precious memories.

Even if you want to walk one of the bigger pilgrimages like the Camino eventually, don't overlook your own country. Lesser-known pilgrimages can be deeply meaningful and are certainly less crowded.

If you choose to travel overseas, then the cost and number of practical preparations will rise accordingly.

Distance and time

There are pilgrimages that take just a day or a weekend, and they are certainly valuable and interesting. But I have found that the challenges of pilgrimage take a little more time to emerge and the benefits of a longer journey lie in overcoming them.

If you are walking and carrying your pack, then it's a good idea to work up to longer distances.

I did the Pilgrims' Way in six days, and the St Cuthbert's Way in five. The Camino Portuguese Coastal route took fourteen days, and I certainly recommend doing shorter walks before tackling it.

I had previously intended to walk the Camino Frances from St-Jean-Pied-de-Port, but that can take five weeks and I couldn't take that much of a break from my business. Some pilgrims complete the Camino in stages, but I wanted to walk a full journey on my trip and finish at the Cathedral in Santiago de Compostela.

Time of year

The season you walk will determine how busy the route is, what the weather will probably be, and the availability and cost of accommodation and food, which is usually higher at busy times.

While walking off-season might be attractive as the ways are quieter, you will likely have more challenging weather, and many places for tourists are closed. I walked in early autumn (September and October) for all my pilgrimages, which suited me because the weather conditions were reasonable, and crowds were lower but hotels and restaurants were still open on the edge of the low season.

Solo or group

I am happily married and walk often with Jonathan, but I also love to walk alone. Part of the challenge of my pilgrimages was to walk solo.

I'll cover more of the pros and cons of solo pilgrimage in the next chapter. If you think you'd prefer to participate in a group tour, you may be restricted to the more well-known routes. If a pilgrimage has the possibility of a tour, it's likely to be busier than one without, which is something to consider if you want to avoid crowds.

Organised or free range

I like to know where I am sleeping every night, so I organised my accommodation in advance. For the Pilgrims' Way and St Cuthbert's Way, I booked everything myself. For the Camino Portuguese Coastal, I used Macs Adventure, who booked all accommodation and also provided a useful mobile app for the route. Macs offer luggage transfer, but I chose to carry mine.

Some pilgrims prefer the free-range approach where you walk as far as you want to each day and then find somewhere to sleep, whether that's a hostel or albergue, local B & B, hotel, or camping.

Budget

You can certainly walk a pilgrimage on a budget, camping or staying in albergues or hostels, and eating basic food along the way. But if you want more choice of accommodation and to be able to sample the local cuisine, then it's worth spending a little more.

I met pilgrims on the Camino who had saved for years for the trip, and the cost can be significant if you walk the longer routes and stay in private rooms. Booking through a tour operator can be cheaper than trying to book places individually, so compare prices and find something that suits you.

But don't let finances stop you making a pilgrimage. Choose one nearer your home, go back to basics in terms of your gear, and work up to something longer. Pilgrimage is a wonderful way to travel as it brings a sense of meaning to the experience, so you may walk more than one over time.

Your pilgrimage, your way

We all have different definitions of challenge, and varying capabilities at particular times in our lives. You must choose the variables for your pilgrimage based on your situation.

For the Camino, choose a route based on how much time you have and how far you want to walk. To be eligible for the Compostela certificate, you must walk the last 100 kilometres, but the longest route, the Via de la Plata, is nearly 1,000 kilometres. The Frances is nearly 800 kilometres and remains the most popular and busy route. However, if you have limited time, there are also shorter ways, like the Ingles, or you can do the final stage of one of the longer routes.

There are many companies who can organise and book accommodation for you, or you can walk independently and stay in hostels or albergues along the way. You can carry your own pack or get luggage transfer and carry a day pack. The time of year and weather on your journey will also affect your experience. The challenge of your pilgrimage will vary depending on these practical elements.

Even though each pilgrim is different, it's hard to resist comparing ourselves to others. You might pass a tired and limping pilgrim one day, only to end up like that yourself the next. You might wish your pack were lighter, or you might judge others for 'only' walking five days instead of a longer route. You might judge yourself for not being fit enough, or for not looking after your feet and getting blisters, or for carrying too much stuff.

But no pilgrim is 'better' than another.

We all have different reasons to walk, and our own unique challenges along the way.

Don't judge other people by your standards and don't judge yourself by theirs. Everyone has their own definition of success and their own journey. Decide what you want to achieve and what you will be happy doing and then make the best of your situation.

There are always people ahead and behind, always people in better or worse shape.

It is your pilgrimage and, as in life, you must walk your own path.

Questions:

- Do you feel called to a particular pilgrimage?
- What pilgrimages are available in your country?
- How far do you want to walk and for how many days?
- How comfortable are you with multi-day walking? How could you work up to it?
- Do you want to walk solo, or with someone else or in a group? Are you drawn to a more popular route or one that's more isolated?
- Do you want to know where you're sleeping each night or are you happy to go free range?
- Do you want to carry your pack or get luggage transfer?
- How will these choices affect your budget?
- Are you walking your own path in life? Are you living by other people's definition of success? How can you walk your own path once more?
- What do you want to achieve on your pilgrimage? How will you keep your personal definition of success in mind during your journey?

1.2 WALKING ALONE OR WITH OTHERS

"Just as alone time can be important for creation (and possible subsequent destruction), it can also be necessary for restoration."

—Stephanie Rosenbloom, *Alone Time*

My personal definition of pilgrimage has always been walking alone on a multi-day route, carrying my own pack. Others go in groups, or have luggage portered to their accommodation. Still others walk day trips, or cycle the whole way. Each pilgrim must choose their own challenge, based on their particular situation, and of course, there are pros and cons of walking solo or with others.

If you walk alone, it's all on you

You make your own decisions, and your own mistakes. You have no one to give up responsibility to.

This is both the major benefit of solo walking, and the aspect that most people fear. Planning and then walking a multi-day trip alone is a great way to prove you can be independent and rely on yourself. You have to figure your way out of situations, whatever they might be.

I walked out of a village one morning on the Pilgrims' Way, and as the path wound steeply uphill across bare fields, I just couldn't go on any longer.

Yes, I was tired, but it was also October 2020, when the world was out of control with the pandemic. I was scared for myself and my family. I read the news each day with a sense of impending doom, and I hadn't slept properly for almost a year. I couldn't see any point in continuing with the pilgrimage.

I couldn't see any point in continuing at all.

I sat down by the edge of the path and wept.

I could have phoned Jonathan and he would have comforted me, but he was not there to carry my pack or suggest a solution. I had to figure it out for myself.

There are times when you want to give up on

every journey — sometimes multiple times. If you are alone, it is all on you.

I pulled out an emergency Snickers bar (which I always have in reserve!) and ate it as I wiped my tears away. Then I hefted my pack on and walked up the hill.

When you are alone, only you can choose to continue. Only you can comfort yourself. You have to find motivation — and the will to walk on cultivates resilience.

The following year, I found myself lost on the St Cuthbert's Way, with only horses and sheep for company — and no mobile phone reception for GPS. I had to navigate back to the path using only my own skills and senses. I ended up walking an extra four kilometres that day, but figuring it out was worth it for the satisfaction of solo achievement.

If you are with someone else, or have a group leader, you give up responsibility for navigation. While you don't have to fear getting lost, you also lose the sense of accomplishment and satisfaction that comes from dealing with such situations.

When walking alone, there are no distractions and no one else to interpret the world

You can figure out what you think, what you find interesting, and what resonates with you.

When you walk with others, it's easy to become distracted by conversation about all kinds of things that take you out of the present moment. You will miss aspects of the world around you, and may be influenced by how others interpret the surroundings.

On a pilgrimage, there are aspects of spirituality that are yours alone, and the influence of others who experience the divine in different ways may detract from your individual response.

Of course, "wherever you go, there you are," as Jon Kabat-Zinn wrote. You might travel to escape a situation in your life, but you cannot escape yourself.

Alone, you can walk at your natural pace, stop when you like, walk more slowly up hills, and take all the time you need

I regularly walk with Jonathan and we have also done walking holidays with small groups, and I always have to adapt my pace. Everyone does, as no one walks in the same way at the same speed.

When walking alone, I can stop when I like to take pictures (and I take a lot of them!). I can head into the bushes for a wee, or walk more slowly up hills. I can take all day to walk, or put my headphones in and crank out the kilometres if I'm tired.

The pilgrim saying "your Camino, your way" emphasises the need to put judgment aside. The pilgrimage challenge is yours alone, and if you walk solo, it is easier to decide what that means.

"Stranger, pass by that which you do not love"

This old pilgrim's advice by an anonymous sage is another aspect of 'your pilgrimage, your way.' You get to decide the places along the route that have meaning for you, and they may not be the same for others you travel with, or those that guidebooks laud as important.

I discovered this while walking the Pilgrims' Way through the South Downs of Kent in England. While walking in nature was certainly restorative, I did not truly love the long stretches of open paths across fields and through woods. They were pleasant, and I needed the respite of nature, for sure, but my passion was reserved for the Gothic cathedrals of Southwark and Canterbury with their soaring naves, their arches and vaults, and their lines of clean stone. Their stark beauty caught my imagination so much more, and that is why I loved walking the Pilgrims' Way.

Some great walking routes are primarily about natural beauty, but pilgrimages are more often through the human-built environment. They pass through towns and cities and ports and places where people have lived — and worshipped — for generations. I love the places where we have made our mark more than those that lie in wilderness.

Only you can decide which aspects of a pilgrimage route resonate with you, and 'pass by those things you do not love.'

When walking solo, you can meet other people, walk together a while, and part ways once more

As a solo walker on a pilgrimage route, you will meet other pilgrims along the way — if you choose to — whereas if you are in a couple or an established group, you don't need to meet others outside your circle as you already have company.

When you walk solo, other pilgrims strike up

conversation and you can choose to walk together for a time, maybe share a coffee or a beer, or tips about the route, or get together at the end of the day for a meal. You can also choose to let them walk on, or indicate that you are not interested in chatting.

On the St Cuthbert's Way after getting lost, I met two middle-aged men walking together — Dave and Keith. Dave was an experienced walker with lean limbs and a tiny pack, and he strode confidently across the landscape. Keith was a bigger man with a heavy pack like mine, and he trailed behind, walking with obvious pain in his gait.

We walked together that day and after Keith fell on the moor, I helped clean his wound with my (under-used) first aid kit. We met up again on the last day to Lindisfarne, and I learned of our mutual interest in theology and the different paths it had taken us. I would have liked to continue our conversation, but our ways diverged, as all pilgrimages do eventually. But these encounters can be memorable even in their brevity.

On the first day of my Camino out of Porto, I met a pilgrim, Caroline, heading in the wrong direction. We walked together off and on to Matasinhos that day and had a coffee overlooking the ocean while she bandaged her blisters, which had emerged after only a few kilometres.

There were others along the Camino — two Irish ladies who were only walking a few days and retired early after one sprained her wrist in a fall on the cobblestones; an Australian couple who called hello each morning as they rushed past with their day packs; a young American woman whose mum walked with her the first few days, then injured her ankle and left her daughter to walk alone; an English couple, Sid and Rose, who had met via internet dating and decided to walk the Camino to get to know each other better; a German backpacker who free ranged the route. I met each along the way and we shared friendly words, then we parted with a wave and a 'Buen Camino.'

I'm an introvert, so I enjoy being alone. In fact, I seek it out. I found the Camino more of a challenge because there were so many people on the way.

If you walk solo and want more people-time, you can find companionship more easily if you stay in hostels or accommodation with shared spaces, rather than in private rooms.

Solitude has a resonance with pilgrimage

Cuthbert was a seventh-century monk who later became Bishop of Lindisfarne. He was sainted after his death because of miracles at his tomb, and is the patron saint of Northumbria in the north-east of England. You can still visit his shrine at Durham Cathedral.

When in need of solitude, Cuthbert withdrew to one of the tiny Farne Islands. He even built a wall around his hut so he could only see the sky as he prayed. He was an educated man with responsibilities to his community, serving the king and court at Bamburgh and leading the monks of Lindisfarne.

But solitude was his solace and his joy, and he went back to his little island alone to die.

Cuthbert balanced solitude and company at different times in his life, and perhaps that is the challenge for us all. To withdraw and be alone sometimes, in order to gain strength to go back into the world.

Questions:

- How do you feel about the prospect of walking solo?
- How do you feel about walking in a group?
- How can you use those feelings to help you make decisions about your pilgrimage?
- How can you walk 'your pilgrimage, your way'?
- How can you tap into what you truly love, rather than relying on the opinions of others?
- How is solitude a part of your life?
  Does it recharge you? How could you incorporate more of it?

Resources:

- *Alone Time: Four Seasons, Four Cities, and the Pleasures of Solitude*
  — Stephanie Rosenbloom
- *St Cuthbert's Way: A Pilgrims' Companion*
  — Mary Low
- *Wherever You Go, There You Are: Mindfulness Meditation for Everyday Life*
  — Jon Kabat-Zinn

1.3 PLANNING THE ROUTE, MAPS, AND NAVIGATION

Planning your pilgrimage adds to the anticipation of the journey, and it can also ease any fears as you learn about the task ahead. This chapter is an overview, and I have included more practical details about each route in the Appendices.

Guidebooks

For my two English pilgrimages, I used the excellent Cicerone guidebooks, *Walking the Pilgrims' Way* by Leigh Hatts, and *Walking St Oswald's Way and St Cuthbert's Way* by Rudolf Abraham.

There are many Camino guides for each route. I used *The Camino Portugués: A Wise Pilgrim Guide* as it was slender and light. I also cut out the pages

I didn't need for my route to reduce the weight further. I also took some pages from *A Pilgrim's Guide to the Camino Portugués* by John Brierley, which added questions to consider and aspects of the cultural and religious settings that the *Wise Pilgrim* guide left out.

Accommodation

If you're traveling with a tour company, they will organise your accommodation. I booked through Macs Adventure for the Camino and was (mostly) happy with the places I stayed each night.

For the Pilgrims' Way and St Cuthbert's Way, I traveled independently and booked my accommodation well in advance. The guidebooks contain some options, but I also used Google Maps to search local places to stay along the route.

It's certainly possible to wild camp, or find somewhere to sleep when you get tired, but as a solo female traveler, I like to have a safe, private room with a bathroom each night, and I also like to know how far I have to walk each day to get there.

The particular challenge of the St Cuthbert's Way

The St Cuthbert's Way has few places to stay on the route, so if you're traveling independently without a tour company, you need to book in advance, especially if you want to walk over the sands to Lindisfarne.

> Once you know the approximate dates you want to walk, check the tide times for your final day's crossing at holyislandcrossingtimes.northumberland.gov.uk.

The tides wait for no pilgrim and you must walk the sands within the safe window, which changes every day. While it is critical to respect the tide and the weather, I highly recommend you walk the sands if conditions are safe enough. It is one of the most memorable walks of my life and a fitting end to the pilgrimage. Crossing on the edge of the busy causeway road or getting a taxi or bus over cannot compare.

If you have an early crossing window, you need to stay close to the coast the night before and there are only a few accommodation options. If you want to stay on Lindisfarne, and I highly recommend that too, you need to book well in advance, as there are only a few places available on the island.

Maps and apps

For my two English routes, I bought the paper Ordnance Survey (OS) Maps specified in the guidebooks. I traced the route in highlighter across the pages, then cut out the sections I needed and folded them into a waterproof map holder to carry with me, discarding the rest.

As part of my preparation, I joined them all up across my living room floor so I could visualise the route.

You can see a photo at
www.jfpenn.com/pilgrimswaymaps

I downloaded the OS Maps app and also mapped the walk on the Komoot app, where you can share walks with others. I planned each day and then shared them with Jonathan, so he knew which route I intended to walk.

For the Camino, I used the Macs Adventure app, which was excellent and included water and public toilets as well as the Camino route.

For all three, I also used Google Maps, particularly

in urban sections, to find recommended places for coffee during the day or to eat in the evenings.

If you are traveling overseas for your pilgrimage, organise mobile roaming or get a local SIM card. Phone and internet access are both useful for GPS and also important from a safety perspective, especially if you are solo walking.

If you're traveling to places where you don't speak the predominant language, consider downloading the Google Translate app and the languages you might need for offline use. You can speak in one language and the app will show text and even read aloud the words in another language. You can also use Google Lens to translate signs and apps, all of which help in the less touristy places. I used both on the Camino in the smaller Portuguese villages along the way.

Navigation on the route

Pilgrimages are generally on established paths and people have been traveling some of them for hundreds of years. Most pilgrimages are well waymarked with a particular symbol representing the route attached to posts, fences, gates, stiles, and trees at regular intervals.

You don't have to navigate much to stay on the

right path, but it's always a good idea to know where you are and if you're walking solo on a less popular route at low season, then navigation is an important aspect of safety.

I did some navigation back when I was in the Girl Guides and I've been on two Outward Bound courses, but I was still apprehensive before my first solo pilgrimage. To counter that fear, I went on a navigation training day through the National Navigation Award Scheme (NNAS) to improve my map-reading skills.

A violent storm rolled in that day, and I was the only student who showed up at a farmyard barn in Wiltshire for the session. With two instructors teaching only me, it was an intense day, but I refreshed my skills at using a compass, reading maps, pacing and distance, as well as safety when walking. I finished the day feeling far more confident in my ability to stay safe and find my way if I got lost.

This navigation training was particularly useful for the St Cuthbert's Way, which had fewer signposts than the Pilgrim's Way and many fewer than the Camino. But the training was more about my confidence than anything else and certainly made me feel more competent as a solo walker.

Planning to visit cultural, religious, and historical places along the route

I enjoy pilgrimage walks, in particular, because their routes encompass places of cultural, religious, and historic significance. I love ancient churches and cathedrals, whether still active or in ruins, and I like to sense what remains in these places of meaning.

If there are particular sites you want to see along the way, then be sure to time your walk so you arrive when they are open — and you still have energy for a visit.

Schedule extra time at the beginning and the end of your journey, so you don't rush those first and last days, and allow more time to see the sites as a tourist without a pack.

For the Pilgrims' Way, it's worth visiting Southwark Cathedral in London and Canterbury Cathedral at the end. For the St Cuthbert's Way, the key sites are Melrose Abbey at the start and Lindisfarne, Holy Island, at the end. For the Camino, I started in Porto, which is a fantastic city, and you need at least a day for Santiago de Compostela after you finish.

There will be other places along the route, but you may not have the energy to visit, or the timing of the day's walk may not allow for it.

On the St Cuthbert's Way, I wanted to visit the ruins of Jedburgh Abbey, founded in the twelfth century and still a beautiful site. But after a gruelling day, I arrived too late the night before, and left before dawn the next morning in a storm. I visited it in the darkness and looked up through the ruins to the night sky above, vowing to return at some point.

It's also worth checking if you need a ticket to visit, as booking in advance has become a lot more common since the pandemic to control visitor numbers. Some places might also be inaccessible.

I had hoped to stay at The Friars, Aylesford Priory, for a night on the Pilgrims' Way. Founded in the thirteenth century, the Carmelite monastery is now a retreat centre and a place of pilgrimage in itself. But when I walked in October 2020, it was closed because of the pandemic, so I wasn't able to stay. The open-air sections and the cafe were still open, and I appreciated their coffee and walnut cake, at least.

While the guidebooks explain many of the significant sites along the route, you will also find places that resonate and remain memorable, even if not considered important by others.

One morning on the Pilgrims' Way, I walked into Boxley, a village on the outskirts of Maidstone in

Kent. The autumn sun was low in the sky and cast a golden light over the gravestones as I arrived at the church of St Mary and All Saints, a place of worship for nearly 800 years. Under the canopy of the ornate lychgate (the roofed gateway to the churchyard) were benches for the faithful to rest, and on one sat a selection of pumpkins and squash, in shades of yellow, orange and green. A handwritten sign urged, "Please help yourself."

I wandered alone in the graveyard, one of my favourite things to do anywhere in the world. Most of the graves were so weathered that the text could no longer be read, a reminder that our names will also be forgotten one day.

Several headstones had sunk deep into the ground, leaning to one side as if they felt the pull of the dark beneath. Wild cyclamens in shades of violet grew beneath a sycamore tree, late flowers of autumn marking new life from the bones of the buried dead.

One boundary wall was straddled by a huge beech tree, which must have started growing over it well before the World War II memorial that lay just on the other side. Our human-made barriers cannot hold nature for long.

I sat in the silence of that peaceful churchyard for a while before walking on. You might find a sparse line or two about that church in the guidebook, but it sticks in my mind as a far more special place.

Planning versus serendipity

Some planning is essential for pilgrimage, but don't overschedule your trip. Leave room for serendipity and the possibility of chance encounters along the way, and certainly allow time at the beginning and end of your trip for reflection.

Questions:

- What resources will you use to research your pilgrimage route?
- Have you booked accommodation and any places of interest or necessary aspects of the trip along the way?
- Are you confident that you will be able to navigate the route? If not, how can you gain that confidence?
- Which spots along the route do you want to spend more time in?
- Have you allowed time for serendipity?

Resources:

- *Walking the Pilgrims' Way* — Leigh Hatts
- *Walking St Oswald's Way and St Cuthbert's Way* — Rudolf Abraham
- *The Camino Portugués: A Wise Pilgrim Guide* — and other guidebooks at www.wisepilgrim.com
- *A Pilgrim's Guide to the Camino Portugués* — John Brierley
- Lindisfarne, Holy Island tide times and safe crossing windows — holyislandcrossingtimes.northumberland.gov.uk
- OS Maps. Physical maps and app available — www.ordnancesurvey.co.uk
- Komoot app — www.komoot.com
- Macs Adventure — www.macsadventure.com
- British Pilgrimage Trust — www.britishpilgrimage.org
- National Navigation Award Scheme (NNAS) — www.nnas.org.uk

"ALL JOURNEYS HAVE SECRET DESTINATIONS *of which the traveler is unaware.*"

MARTIN BUBER

1.4 PHYSICAL PREPARATION AND TRAINING

While you can just set out with a pack into the dawn, your pilgrimage will be a better experience if you physically prepare for it in some way. How you choose to train will depend on your overall health and fitness, as well as how much time you have before your journey.

You can walk a pilgrimage without specialist training or super fitness

I am not a tough solo adventurer by any means, and you don't need to be in order to walk most pilgrimage journeys, but you do need to be able to get up and walk every day for several days in a row.

When I walked The Pilgrims' Way, I was forty-five,

slightly overweight, with no experience walking solo over multiple days.

For the St Cuthbert's Way, I was forty-six, slightly more overweight, and recovering from a bout of COVID-19 that left me struggling for breath more often than usual.

For the Camino de Santiago, I was forty-seven, slightly less overweight, but certainly not a racing snake by any means.

You can walk these pilgrimages as a 'normal person,' but I would definitely recommend multi-day, back-to-back walking to train for the longer Camino routes, so you get used to the kilometres involved.

I am able-bodied but I saw pilgrims with disabilities on the Camino, and there are organisations listed in the resources section that can support those with physical or mental challenges.

Walk in preparation

If you want to do a long walking pilgrimage, presumably you like to walk already, and the best way to prepare is to walk more.

On the Camino, I met pilgrims who had never walked long days before and had never done a multi-day walk. They suffered greatly from the lack of experience and this is one reason that many leave the way.

I walk regularly for pleasure and exercise and for many years, we did not have a car, so I often walked eight to ten kilometres on a 'normal' day, and around twenty on a longer weekend walk.

I lift weights and work out with a personal trainer twice a week, and strengthening my leg muscles definitely helped prevent the knee issues I witnessed in others on the Camino.

Over the last decade, I've been on group walking holidays led by a guide. I've also done several ultra-marathon walks of 50 kilometres in one day, and I've walked 100 kilometres in a weekend (50 kilometres each on back-to-back days). But before the Pilgrims' Way, I had never walked six days in a row carrying a full pack, let alone walked solo on a route I didn't know.

Training for a longer walk means allocating more time for it, and the days are repetitive as you are often walking the same route multiple times instead of an end-to-end journey. But it's worth doing to strengthen your muscles, get used to your gear, and to experience walking when tired, and potentially in pain, before you tackle the pilgrimage itself.

If possible, train for the terrain and the weather you might experience

Walking on flat, hard ground for long distances is very different from walking up and down steep, boggy hills. Walking in autumnal storms and icy winds is very different from walking in summer heat and humidity.

The terrain and weather will impact your walking speed, as well as what gear you need. If possible, it's a good idea to test your gear in some of the conditions you expect to encounter, or at least try to anticipate their impact on your pilgrimage.

Questions:

- What physical training and preparation will you undertake for your pilgrimage?
- What kinds of terrain and weather do you expect, and how can you replicate them in your training?
- Are you confident that you can get up and walk each day? If not, how will you gain this confidence?

Resources:

- The Camino with reduced mobility — https://www.pilgrim.es/en/plan-your-way/reduced-mobility
- Confraternity of St James details for pilgrims with disabilities — www.csj.org.uk/faqs/pilgrims-with-disabilities

1.5 WHAT TO TAKE WITH YOU — AND WHAT TO LEAVE BEHIND

> "Walking manages to free us from our illusions about the essential."
>
> —Frédéric Gros, *A Philosophy of Walking*

The amount you carry will directly affect your experience of pilgrimage. The less you carry, the lighter your pack, the less weight on your feet, the easier the walk, the less pain you will have.

I've listed my kit from the Camino in Appendix 5, but my lessons learned are below.

Consider luggage transfer

If you want to make things easier, or if you have constraints that prevent you from carrying your own pack, you can get luggage transfer on many of the pilgrimage routes. This may be an option with the company you book with, or you can arrange it privately with local companies.

If you carry a bigger pack, you will fill it

I made the mistake of carrying too much on the Pilgrims' Way and also the St Cuthbert's Way. It was cold and wet weather so I needed heavier waterproofs and warm clothing, but I carried way too much stuff, and could only do so because I had a bigger pack (50 litres).

My need for more 'stuff' was partly because of my fear of not being prepared for every eventuality. I had way too many pairs of socks and T-shirts because I didn't think I'd be able to wash anything en route. I had a huge first aid kit, too much back-up food, and I even took my iPad on the Pilgrims' Way in case I had to work, which I swiftly regretted.

For the Camino, I learned my lesson and carried an Osprey Sirrus 36-litre pack with an in-built raincover, which was perfect.

Use walking poles

Walking poles are not just for those with bad knees, and in fact, if you use them while fit, you might prevent injury.

I love my walking poles! They help me balance on rocky and uneven ground and provide extra help on steep slopes. I can use them to probe puddles and cross streams. They help me get into a rhythm on longer walks, and keep my fingers from swelling up, plus they keep this tired and wobbly pilgrim from stumbling towards the end of the day.

If you're flying, you will need to check in your walking poles. I used LEKI Women's Micro Vario Carbon Trekking Poles for the Camino. They are really light and fold into three pieces so I could fit them in my pack for the flight.

If you're going to use poles, learn how to walk with them beforehand. Your hands should rest in the slings so you don't have to grip too hard, and this encourages a more natural swing. You also need to adjust the length for your height and gait. Ask someone to show you or watch one of the many videos on YouTube. I walked incorrectly with poles for years before someone showed me the proper way and it made all the difference.

Waterproofs and dry bags

You will get wet on a multi-day walk. It is almost inevitable. How wet you get will be based on your gear, and how miserable you are will be based on your attitude.

You can go hardcore on your waterproofs, with heavy trousers, gaiters, boots and socks, jackets, ponchos, and more. But all this will affect the weight you carry, and I definitely took too much on my St Cuthbert's pilgrimage.

Ponchos are great in principle as they cover you and your pack, leaving no gap behind your neck. But in practice, rain often comes with wind and unless you bind the poncho around you, it billows and is more annoying than anything else. I wore a bright yellow poncho over my usual waterproofs in the driving rain on the St Cuthbert's along a particular stretch of road for visibility, but it was too heavy, and I should have left it behind.

You can buy dry bags of different sizes. I kept my clothes in one inside my pack under the waterproof pack cover. I also had a small one for my phone, which I kept inside my jacket pocket, or in a small hip bag.

Walking shoes or boots + another pair

I usually prefer walking shoes to boots for the lighter weight and less rubbing around my ankles. I wore walking shoes (KEEN or Merrell) on all three routes, but if you are doing the St Cuthbert's Way in bad weather or winter conditions, then boots would be better, especially across the Cheviot (pronounced 'chee-vee-ot') Hills, which can be boggy.

I saw some pilgrims walking in heavy boots on the Camino, but they were unnecessary for the terrain, especially if you have walking poles for any rocky, wet, or uneven ground.

I crossed the sands to Holy Island wearing my walking shoes and waterproof socks. Some walk barefoot, but I had blisters and didn't want to risk hurting my feet further. Once I was on land again, I put my muddy, wet shoes in a bag and washed and dried them at the B & B later.

For every pilgrimage, you need something to wear in the evening once you take your shoes or boots off. I took a lightweight pair of trainers on the Pilgrims' Way and St Cuthbert's Way, and sandals on the Camino.

You can buy (most of) what you need on the route

Pilgrimage walks pass through villages, towns, and even cities along the way. You will generally be able to get to a supermarket, pharmacy, restaurant or cafe, and bar every day, and in some places, there will be bigger shops catering to travellers with even more to purchase.

You don't need to bring an enormous bottle of shampoo or loads of toiletries for every possibility. You can buy more on the route. Only the St Cuthbert's Way had sparse options in some places, but even then, I found food stops every day.

Technology as an aid — or a crutch?

Pilgrimage can be the ideal opportunity for a digital fast, a time to turn off the constant stream of the internet and stop consuming online news, podcasts, articles, social media, TV and music. Time to see the world through your own senses, rather than a screen.

I'll readily admit to having my phone within reach at all times. I am an augmented-human and I use technology in every part of my life. But I also know that doom-scrolling makes me miserable and that I am happiest walking a trail with nothing but the sound of birdsong and my footsteps on the path.

On longer multi-day pilgrimages, time slows. Life becomes simpler and all that matters is walking, eating, and sleeping.

I didn't actively decide on digital minimalism before my Camino. It just happened that way. I checked my email in the morning and evening and posted once a day on social media, as I have an online business and I needed to keep things ticking over while I traveled. But I didn't listen to podcasts, and I triaged my email, saving anything non-urgent for my return. Nothing seemed that important after a day's walk. Everything else falls away when you're tired.

However, my phone was absolutely necessary for safety and navigation purposes, as well as finding coffee and food off the path, as outlined in Chapter 1.3 on maps and apps. I think a phone with an internet connection is important to have on a longer pilgrimage, but set some boundaries for yourself around how much you want to use it beyond what you need for the journey.

What else are you carrying?

Baggage is not just physical. There are plenty of other kinds of emotional and spiritual baggage you might carry with you, and they too might affect your experience.

These might include expectations of what you want to happen physically or spiritually; judgment of yourself or other pilgrims; intolerance of local food, accommodation, and customs; fear and worry about the journey or what you have left behind; and many other things.

While you consider slimming down your physical luggage, make sure to spend time on what other baggage you can leave behind.

Questions:

- How will you stop yourself from taking too much stuff?
- Have you walked in your full gear as practice before leaving?
- How will you use your phone on pilgrimage?
- What emotional and spiritual baggage can you leave behind?

Resources:

- See Appendix 5 for my gear and kit list recommendations

WHAT ELSE ARE YOU CARRYING?

What could you leave behind?

1.6 PREPARING FOR THE INNER JOURNEY

"Walking can provoke these excesses: surfeits of fatigue that make the mind wander, abundances of beauty that can turn the soul over… Walking ends by awakening this rebellious, archaic part of us."

—Frédéric Gros, *A Philosophy of Walking*

While the practical side is a critical part of preparation, pilgrimage is also a chance to take an inner journey. If you just want a long walk, there are plenty of natural trails, but pilgrimage provides a chance to go deeper.

Once you start your pilgrimage, the physical routine of walking, finding food, water, and shelter takes over. The deeper thoughts you expected to have can fall away in the face of heat, cold, or rain, as well as fatigue and pain.

But when you stop in the shade of a tree in the heat of the afternoon, or lie with your feet up at the end of the day, there is a chance to ponder the deeper aspects of pilgrimage.

Clear the decks and slow down

Clear space in your schedule for the few weeks before your journey, so you have time to consider what you want your pilgrimage to be. Journal about it, or pray if you are a person of faith. Prepare your mind and spirit as well as your body for the journey.

In the last few days, slow down and shift into pilgrim time, where life is simpler. Perhaps do a digital detox and stop watching the cycle of news and social media so you can disconnect from your usual routines.

I like to physically clear my desk, de-clutter, and clean my office before I leave, putting away my computer so my mind knows it's time to leave that side of me behind.

Questions to consider on pilgrimage

I take a journal to write in, and I print out and stick a list of questions in the front to think about on the way. You can adapt the following list to your pilgrimage or write your own.

You don't need to answer every question, and others may emerge for you. Some will even seem unimportant later. But at least they may help set your intentions for this period of contemplation and remind you to set aside time for inner explorations. Otherwise time could pass quickly on the journey, and you may miss the chance to think.

You can download a printable list at www.jfpenn.com/pilgrimagedownload

What am I escaping from?

What am I seeking?

What am I curious about?

What do I notice in the world around me? Consider all the senses. What do I see, hear, smell, taste, touch — and also with my inner self — what do I feel inside? What resonates?

What is my challenge today? What is difficult? What do I need to overcome? Where is the gift in the hardship?

What am I afraid of?

What am I disappointed about? How can I reframe the situation?

What surprised me? What delighted me? What brought me joy?

How did serendipity creep into my plan? How can I leave room for more of it?

If I look at the world with the eyes of a stranger, what is interesting? Where can I find wonder? How can I embrace beginner's mind?

What is the history of this place and how does it resonate now?

What is ancient, and what is modern? What is the same, and what has changed?

What is the truth behind the monuments? What is the alternate history?

What is permanent? What is transient?

Memento mori. Remember, you will die. How can I keep this in mind today? What underscores this along the way?

What do I take for granted?

What do I need to reinvent?

How do I feel physically? Emotionally? Spiritually?

What is nagging at me? What do I need to sort out?

What can I let go of? What can I release?

How can I live more simply?

How can I stop looking down at my feet on the path? How can I remember to look up… then further up?

I don't want to get lost — but what if I'm meant to get lost? What are the benefits of being lost sometimes?

What do I want to share about the journey? What can I keep secret just for me?

"Stranger, pass by that which you do not love." What should I pass by? What do I love?

How do I want to live? How can I serve others while doing that?

What is faith to me? What do I believe in? What makes this a pilgrimage rather than just a long walk?

Where is the shadow or the darkness here? Where is the 'under-glimmer' as the poet Bashō called it? How can I experience this journey more deeply?

What is the transformation of this journey?

PILGRIMAGE

How am I a pilgrim? A wanderer? A curious soul who crosses boundaries?

What is sacred? What is profane? What is divine? What is human?

Where is the veil thin?

Where am I ripped thin enough to feel it?

Questions:

- How will you prepare for the inner journey of pilgrimage before your departure?
- Will you set aside time each day for reflection during the pilgrimage? Do you plan to bring along a journal or another system for capturing your thoughts?
- What questions resonate with you?
- Can you add some of your own?

Resources:

- Printable list of questions at www.jfpenn.com/pilgrimagedownload
- *The Art of Pilgrimage: The Seeker's Guide to Making Travel Sacred* — Phil Cousineau

1.7 FACING FEARS

> "The dangers of life are infinite,
> and among them is safety."
>
> —Johann Wolfgang von Goethe

Life is about balancing risk — and so, in a tiny way, is a solo pilgrimage, even if you're walking along established routes and staying in pre-booked accommodation each night.

Pilgrimages are generally not wilderness walks and do not cross extreme terrains where physical safety is more of an issue, but regardless, you will probably have fears before your journey. I certainly did!

Preparation is the best way to avoid trouble, so I wrote down my concerns before leaving and found ways to mitigate them as much as possible. Often our fears about something happening are greater than the actual event, if it even happens, but it's good to consider in advance what you might do, just in case.

The benefits of pilgrimage are worth stretching yourself for, so don't let your fears stop you.

Here are some of my fears and others that might concern you.

Fear of getting lost

This is a natural concern, especially when walking solo, but most pilgrimages are well way-marked and, depending on the route and season you walk, there will be other pilgrims ahead of you on the way. While other people might be useful for reference, don't follow blindly, as I saw pilgrims heading off in the wrong direction several times on the Camino.

I found the Pilgrims' Way a perfect first route as a novice navigator and as my first solo multi-day walk. Much of the way is on established paths and trails and it's well-signposted. You're never too far from civilisation, so you don't need to carry anything more than basic supplies. There are coffee shops, cafes, and pubs along the route and plenty of B & Bs and hotels, so you don't need to camp. You can get a taxi or a train or a bus from many points if you decide to stop walking or need help.

But of course, I didn't know that before setting out!

I mitigated my fear by doing National Navigation Award Scheme (NNAS) training, as well as detailed route planning with the guidebook and physical OS Maps. I carried my phone in a small dry-bag with Google Maps and the OS Maps app and an external battery for charging during the day. I used Google Maps at several points, particularly in built-up urban areas, when it was harder to navigate the physical map due to scale.

Despite all my planning and preparation, I got lost a few times on the Pilgrims' Way, but only for a short time. At one point, I ended up wandering around a strawberry farm until I found a tiny path at the side of an overgrown hedge which had covered the way-marker.

I also took an unnecessary route through some gritty housing estates on the outskirts of east London towards Dartford. But neither experience was a big deal, and it became part of the challenge. On one estate in London, a teenage girl stopped me, her eyes wide with surprise. She said she had never seen anyone with such a big backpack and said she felt tired even just walking up the stairs in her house. She couldn't believe I was walking for so many days, and I like to think perhaps I inspired her a little. But I was clearly off the route that day!

The St Cuthbert's Way was more challenging, and I had to use more active navigation skills in places where the way-markers were more spaced out, and sometimes missing altogether or on the reverse side of posts.

On a narrow stretch of path, a couple of dog walkers stood aside to let me pass. I continued down to a waterfall and then (unthinkingly) crossed the river and walked on through several fields before checking the map and realising I was off course. I was in a valley and there was no phone signal and I only had a vague idea of where I was.

I should have turned around and retraced my steps, but I thought I could circle back up to the path. I did circle back, but in the opposite direction, so I walked a few extra kilometres that day. On the second time around, after meeting fellow pilgrims Dave and Keith, I discovered that the dog walkers had stood in front of the way-marker.

Fear of other people

This is not something I generally worry about because I love walking alone and have done it often in my own country as well as traveling solo abroad. But as I shared pictures on Instagram @jfpennauthor each day, several women asked whether I was anxious walking alone or whether I feared being attacked, so I wanted to cover it here.

The Pilgrims' Way was quiet, especially in autumn 2020, when people were staying home because of the pandemic. I was alone most of the time outside of urban areas, and the only people I saw were dog walkers or fellow hikers, friendly people who love their solitude as much as I do. We nodded or said hello, but there wasn't much interaction on the way. As an introvert, I was happy with that.

The St Cuthbert's Way was even quieter. I walked alone for most of the time, and the few people I did meet were fellow pilgrims. The Camino de Santiago was quite the opposite in that it was busy with pilgrims every day, so it was difficult to walk alone.

The media stoke fear of others, highlighting tragic and violent events, but in my travels over the decades, much of it alone, I have rarely felt unsafe. Of course, I've had my share of difficult encounters, but they have usually been in bars and other urban settings rather than out walking in the sun and the wind and the rain. People are mostly lovely and will help a stranger, as you would help someone in need.

However, I am cautious and sensible. For each of my pilgrimages, I walked in daylight and made sure to reach my accommodation each night before dark. I planned my itinerary in advance and gave copies to

Jonathan and my mum, so they knew where I was. I shared my location with Jonathan on my phone so he could see where I was real-time, and texted during the day, plus I called every evening.

I also walk with confidence, even with a backpack on. My hard-working single mum drilled this into me as a child because I would walk home alone from school. She took me and my brother to Tang Soo Do martial arts classes where the instructor taught us to 'walk like a predator, not like prey.' I've never forgotten that advice. If you feel like prey when walking alone, consider taking self-defence classes to help with confidence.

While these pilgrimages are mostly safe and away from main roads and traffic, there is some danger from people in cars on the roads. There are places where routes cross or link with sections of road with limited visibility, especially at dawn or dusk.

I walked the Pilgrims' Way in the autumn when twilight came early and the only time I was scared was walking into traffic at dusk, where there was no footpath. I wore a head torch and later bought reflective patches so I was more visible. Make sure drivers can see you, and get off the road as fast as possible when you hear a vehicle approaching. This is less of a problem if you're walking during summer months with longer days.

Fear of COVID-19, illness, and pain

In October 2020, when I walked the Pilgrims' Way, I wasn't afraid of other people physically harming me, but I was walking during a pandemic. We had all been taught to fear other people coughing or even breathing anywhere near us and the fear was palpable, with people veering away or turning their backs to avoid sharing air. I was staying in accommodation along the route and eating in pubs or cafes, so it was possible that I would meet the virus in some form.

Looking back now, the number of cases in the UK were nowhere near what they would be later in the pandemic, but at the time, the fear of the virus was rampant and it was before vaccination reduced the risk of severe disease and death.

I absolutely had reservations about going, but my risk profile as a reasonably fit forty-five-year-old woman with no underlying health conditions was low. My mental health situation was more serious at the time and my need to get away was greater than my fear of illness.

For most of that first pilgrimage, I interacted with so few people I could almost forget the pandemic, and that was a relief in itself. I was outside on my own in the fresh air, and when I went into a shop, cafe, hotel, or B & B, I followed all the requirements around wearing a mask, sanitising, hand-washing, and social distancing.

I caught COVID-19 in July 2021, so by the time I walked the St Cuthbert's Way later that October, I had been vaccinated and also had a level of natural immunity. For the Camino in 2022, the world was learning to live with the virus and it was less of a concern, and certainly not a fear for me anymore.

In more general terms, we all get sick sometimes and being in another country means different food and water, as well as different strains of common diseases. I carried basic painkillers, Imodium for quick relief of diarrhoea, antihistamines for bites and stings, as well as electrolyte powder for dehydration. I used the latter on several hot and sweaty days on the Camino.

In terms of preparing for any other health issues, two of my pilgrimages were in the UK. I knew I could get to a doctor or hospital easily if necessary, and I could also be home within half a day. For the Camino, I had a UK Global Health Insurance Card (GHIC) and I also have private travel insurance.

Even if you don't get sick, some kind of physical pain from the exertion of walking long days, multiple days in a row with a full pack, is (almost) inevitable. While I expected a certain amount of stiffness and aches, I was worried about hurting myself in a more serious fashion before the Pilgrims' Way.

I had to walk between twenty-five and forty-two kilometres per day and I had never carried my bigger pack for an entire trip, plus I had not walked six days in a row before. I was alone, so what if I fell and twisted my ankle or broke my leg? What if I had such terrible blisters, I couldn't walk?

To counteract these fears, I trained for the distance and was careful to walk with poles when the ground was muddy or uneven to prevent a fall.

You can further mitigate risks in the following ways:

Prepare for the route and expected weather conditions

When you step out on pilgrimage, you must embrace the elements. You have to be ready for what might come based on the particular route and season, but you also have to adapt to the situation.

For the St Cuthbert's Way in the north-east of England in the autumn, I carried full wet weather gear and extra layers for warmth, whereas for the Camino at a similar time, it was mostly warm and I only carried a light waterproof and wore quick-dry shorts.

I had several full days of rain and storms on all three routes, some freezing mornings on the St Cuthbert's Way, and some sweltering days on the Camino. You cannot control the weather, you can only prepare for it.

Use technology, but have analogue backups just in case

For all three pilgrimages, I used navigation apps on the route, but also carried a paper guidebook and maps.

I carried an external battery for my phone so I could charge it on the walk. I needed it several times, so it was worth the extra weight.

If you use the Komoot app, you can share the route with others, so I shared all my walks with Jonathan. We also have a family Apple account so he could see where I was in real-time using the Find My (wife) function.

Ask other people for help if you need it

While there were stretches of each route where I walked alone without seeing people for a while, all pilgrimages (outside of the depths of winter) have other people walking the way. They are pilgrims like you, or people who live in the area. If you need help, ask for it. Most people will help a pilgrim in need.

> "Resilience is the ability to regulate one's response to fear."
> —Barbara Bradley Hagerty, *Life Reimagined*

Questions:

- What are you afraid of? Write down everything big and small, rational and irrational.
- How can you mitigate those fears?
- You can never get rid of all your fear. Is it worth going on pilgrimage anyway?

Resources:

- Check your country's government site before traveling. UK Government travel advice per country which includes COVID-19 and other disease risk
  — www.gov.uk/foreign-travel-advice
- UK Global Health Insurance Card — www.nhs.uk/using-the-nhs/healthcare-abroad/apply-for-a-free-uk-global-health-insurance-card-ghic/
- *Life Reimagined: The Science, Art, and Opportunity of Midlife* — Barbara Bradley Hagerty

1.8 THE DAY BEFORE: SOUTHWARK, LONDON

You can prepare all you like, but at some point, you have to leave.

This is my journal entry for the day before my first pilgrimage.

Bath, England — 15 October 2020

The day before starting the Pilgrims' Way

I wake before dawn as the wind howls outside. The tail end of a storm lashes the trees on the ridge line outside my window, like the sound of the ocean roaring onto a distant shore.

As the sun rises and the storm passes, clouds scud across the pale blue sky over the valley. I want to rise and fly with them. I want to be out there on the path, pack on my back, eyes fixed on the horizon.

Today I will escape these four walls.

PILGRIMAGE

I walk out the door into a crisp autumn morning and the sun is a blessing as I head down the hill into town to get the train to London. I'm careful on the steep path, wary of the slippery leaves by the community garden as the wind whips more from the trees, whirling around me in shades of orange and brown.

I should probably use my walking poles on the uneven ground, but this is still central Bath and I would look like an idiot. I'm already out of place in this suburb with my walking gear and backpack. It's a relief because I'm tired of fitting in, being quiet, laying low, staying inside.

The solid weight of my pack sits tight around my hips and I feel a quickening within as I lengthen my stride. I'm only leaving for a week, but it feels every bit as exciting as when I left the UK for Perth, Australia, back in the year 2000. My pack then contained everything I owned and leaving was exquisite freedom. I didn't know it as I walked away back then, but I had started a new life and it would be eleven years before I moved back to the UK.

Setting off on a journey can have unexpected consequences that shape the path of our lives. I may have a destination in mind for this pilgrimage, but I hope it might also give me back the freedom I desperately need once more.

Back then, I left nothing behind. I was twenty-five and single, with only a little money in the bank. I gave up my job, and I had no responsibilities at all.

Today, I'm walking away from my husband, my best friend, who I will text within the hour and return to in a week. I'm happy in my marriage and I have work that I love. Bath is my home and I don't want to start a whole new life. What I need is to move across the face of the world and feel alive again.

Shut up inside for so much of this pandemic year, I've experienced too much of the world through a screen and the skewed lens of the media has contorted my mind into spiralling catastrophe. My world has shrunk. The walls press in and domestic routine has atrophied my creative soul. I need to get out before what is already fragile splinters and cracks beyond repair.

The train is almost empty, but even so, I adjust my mask, pulling it tighter as the reminder to social distance keeps travellers in their seats.

PILGRIMAGE

In London, the Underground is deserted as I head for Southwark. There are no tourists, no flights, no travel. Most people are working from home if they can. Shops and restaurants are closed or have severe restrictions. Much of the world is sheltering in place and part of me feels I should be, too.

I walk out of the station and the few people on the street hurry past, mostly masked, a palpable fear in the air. No one meets your eyes in London at normal times, but now, the avoidance of direct gaze feels furtive and accusatory, as if by merely breathing, I am a transgressor.

The city is empty, almost apocalyptic. I have never seen the capital so quiet. London moves to Level 2 tomorrow, with no mixing of households indoors. I can only hope we won't have another complete lockdown, but I fear the bars of the cage will slam shut once more before long.

I have spent the pandemic so far lying low, trying not to be a burden. If I can avoid the virus and stay healthy, then precious resources can be spent on those who need it. But I can't lie low any longer. I need to get out into the world before the bitter weather sets in and winter traps us inside for months.

I walk past Borough Market, usually bustling with the smells of hog roast and mulled cider, while the calls of market vendors selling wild mushrooms or artisan sourdough echo up to the rafters. But the pleasure of a slow walk through the market, stopping to sample delicious treats, is gone. The stalls are shuttered; the pubs are empty, and the only smell is antiseptic hand sanitiser.

No touch. No taste. No smell.

The world has lost its senses.

Something is dying, or perhaps has already died here. London will always be reborn, but now is the season of death.

I'm suddenly overwhelmed by the need to go home to Jonathan and be safe together in our home — or die together, if that is what must come. Everything feels so uncertain and the reality of being here hits me.

What if I've made a terrible mistake coming away alone?

What if I pay too high a price for my desperate need for freedom?

I stop myself from heading back into the Underground and fleeing the city. I check into the hotel, take off my pack, and review the maps I have carefully prepared for my route each day. It helps to see that I'm not too far from home. I can get back to Bath in a few hours if I need to, but I have to go on this journey.

PILGRIMAGE

I have been enmeshed with Jonathan in our house for months and our routine has become embedded after so long at home. We have worn grooves in our shared life that feel happily familiar but could easily turn into ruts that deepen so much I can't climb out. We are closer than ever and it's hard to stretch the bonds of our marriage when they are so tight. But I need to push my boundaries once again or I will become just one half of a whole, and that is not what we intended our marriage to be.

In our wedding ceremony back in 2008, we included a verse from the poet Kahlil Gibran. We vowed we would "stand together yet not too near together: For the pillars of the temple stand apart, And the oak tree and the cypress grow not in each other's shadow." This pandemic time has entwined our roots and our branches, and I don't know if I can stand apart any longer. I need to prove that I can.

There are a few hours left of the day, so I visit Southwark Cathedral, a place of worship for over a thousand years, and the starting point of the Pilgrims' Way.

A woman kneels in a pew praying quietly and candles flicker in front of an altar. I want to buy a pilgrim passport but the cathedral shop is closed. I want to find someone to give me a pilgrim's blessing, but there is no one to ask.

I light a candle and think of my family. I send them love and ask a God I don't believe in to keep them safe from this plague. There is something about collective faith that sinks into ancient stones such as these, and perhaps the candle smoke can pass more easily through the veil here, carrying my words to the divine. It might be a meaningless gesture, but it calms me as I stand alone in this cold place surrounded by a thousand years of death.

The tombs of the wealthy lie here, but the shadow of this extravagant faith is a few streets away at Crossbones Graveyard. While the rich have ornate tombs in the cathedral, the outcast dead lie in unmarked graves on unconsecrated land. Dirty ribbons tied to the metal gates mark their passing alongside plastic Madonna figures and memorial signs made from cheap plywood with handwritten felt-tip hearts.

As I walk back to the hotel, I notice graffiti art on a brick wall. A skull wears a blue surgical mask, death trying to hold back death.

I can't control what's happening in the world. But I can put one foot in front of the other and walk my pilgrimage. Perhaps that is enough to anchor me in the dark days ahead.

Resources:

- Southwark (pronounced Suth-uk) is a special place for me and forms the backdrop to my Brooke and Daniel crime thrillers: *Desecration*, *Delirium*, and *Deviance* — www.jfpenn.com/brookeanddaniel
- I've also written articles and shared photos about the area on my Books and Travel site. Southwark Cathedral, London — www.booksandtravel.page/southwark-cathedral
- Crossbones Graveyard, London — www.booksandtravel.page/crossbones
- Walk the South Bank of the Thames from Tower Bridge to Westminster, London — www.booksandtravel.page/walk-south-bank
- London: A Personal History. A solo episode of my Books and Travel Podcast with pictures and transcript if you prefer to read — www.booksandtravel.page/london-a-personal-history

PART 2:
THE JOURNEY

2.1 THE PILGRIM'S DAY

> "When you walk, the world has neither present nor future: nothing but the cycle of mornings and evenings. Always the same thing to do all day: walk."
>
> —Frédéric Gros, *A Philosophy of Walking*

Once you are on the trail — whichever one you choose — the pilgrim's day is much the same.

Wake up, wash, and get dressed.

Check your feet. If necessary, tape and plaster blisters as best you can before putting socks and walking shoes or boots on.

Take painkillers if you need to.

Pack your bag.

Eat breakfast.

Walk.

Stop for coffee, food, or beer depending on the time of day and facilities en route.

Walk, maybe alone, maybe with others.

Arrive at your accommodation.

Shower while washing your sweaty clothes.

Check your feet. Dress blisters and take painkillers if you need to.

Eat dinner, maybe alone, maybe with others.

Rest and sleep.

This daily repetition is one of the blessings of pilgrimage

It simplifies life to its basics.

You have no purpose but to get up and walk.

If you make it to your destination for the night, you have achieved your goal. Tomorrow you will get up and do it again.

But this daily repetition is also part of the challenge.

Even if the way is beautiful, the landscape will remain the same for much of the journey. Another field. Another hill. Another coastal path. Another wood.

If the weather is too hot and sunny, or too wet and miserable, you will trudge through it for hours, regardless.

You will eat mostly the same food every day.

You will tire of wearing the same clothes and having to wash them every night.

You will count your steps on longer days, or sing snippets of song to keep yourself going.

You might walk with another pilgrim for a while, then walk on or let them continue without you. It's rare to find someone who exactly matches your pace, and part of pilgrimage is finding your own stride.

There are small moments of joy in the day. When the rain clears and the sun brightens a corner of the sky, creating a rainbow over the hills. When you find an unexpected coffee shop with delicious local pastries, or appreciate a cold beer in the heat of the day. When you reach your room for the night and take off your walking boots with a sigh of relief. When you have a hot shower to wash off the sweat.

Happiness can come from the simplest things, that which we take for granted in daily life and barely notice until they become the touchstones of the day.

Questions:

- How might the daily repetition of pilgrimage help you?
- Which parts of the pilgrim's day do you expect to find the most challenging?
- What brings you small moments of joy?

Resources:

- *A Philosophy of Walking* — Frédéric Gros

2.2 WALKING IN THE PATH OF HISTORY PUTS LIFE IN PERSPECTIVE

"Nothing ever is, everything is becoming…
All things are passing and nothing abides."

—Heraclitus

On each of my three pilgrimages, I encountered places where I was aware of walking through history, where there was a sense of life being but a brief flash of light across the span of time. My passing on each route was momentary, but pilgrims have walked the same ways for hundreds of years and will continue to walk for generations to come.

The three historic cathedrals are must-visit locations — Southwark Cathedral and Canterbury Cathedral on the Pilgrims' Way, and the Cathedral of Santiago de Compostela at the end of the Camino.

Each has their splendours, and it's worth allowing extra time to visit them. In the same way, the ruined abbey of Lindisfarne and its associated church are insights into history — but these are all obvious highlights.

Here are some other places where I felt a historical perspective.

Mosaic mural on the Old Kent Road, London, England

The first day's walk on the Pilgrims' Way from Southwark Cathedral is through gritty, urban sprawl along a main road, dense with traffic. It might not look like much, but this is the Old Kent Road, originally built by the Romans, linking London to the coast near Dover, and later renamed Watling Street by the Anglo-Saxons.

At a busy corner with Peckham Park Road, under the overhanging porch of the Everlasting Arms Ministry, lies a gigantic thousand-square-foot mosaic mural. *The History of Old Kent Road* by Adam Kossowski has separate panels, each portraying an era of history. The foundation of the city by Romans in their togas surrounded by soldiers with military standards, then medieval London with Chaucer's pilgrims heading for Canterbury and a quote from the poem. King Henry V rides in triumph along the road after the battle of Agincourt, followed by the rebellion of Jack Cade against the government. King Charles II reclaims the throne in the next panel, and then modern London emerges with its British 'bobby' policeman, Pearly Kings and Queens with their mother-of-pearl button suits, and the factories of the city with modern cars driving along.

The mural encapsulates two thousand years of history and yet most pass by without realising that the stones they drive over or walk along have witnessed such historical events.

The artist himself represents another aspect of modern history. Adam Kossowski was Polish and arrived in the UK as a refugee from the Soviet labour camps in 1943. As well as this mural, he created many other artistic works, including the *History of the Carmelites of Aylesford*, at the abbey, which also lies on the Pilgrims' Way and where he was buried after his death in 1986.

You can find pictures at
www.jfpenn.com/oldkentroadmural

Lesnes Abbey, London, England

The ruins of twelfth-century Lesnes Abbey (pronounced 'lane') lie on the Pilgrims' Way in an ancient woodland in east London. Founded in 1178 by the Chief Justiciar to Henry II, it may have been part of a penance to atone for the murder of Archbishop Thomas Becket.

After the Dissolution of the Monasteries in the sixteenth century, the abbey fell into ruin and was eventually lost to farmland before being restored in modern times. The ruins now feature much-appreciated public toilets and a cafe along the Green Chain Walk that forms part of the Pilgrims' Way.

There is a memorial of three triple archways that overlook the ruins, and an ancient mulberry tree with the skyscrapers of the city of London framed on the horizon.

The mulberry tree represents patience, as it will not bud until there is no danger of frost. Its red berries also represent sacrifice, as depicted by Shakespeare's forbidden lovers Pyramis and Thisbe, who died under a mulberry bush, their blood staining the berries red.

Lesnes Abbey is a place of ancient nature and medieval faith against a backdrop of modern London. Well worth a visit.

You can find pictures at
www.jfpenn.com/lesnesabbey

The cadaver tombs of Southwark and Canterbury Cathedrals, England

There are unusual cadaver tombs in both Southwark and Canterbury Cathedral, at the beginning and the end of the Pilgrims' Way. These are rare depictions of the deceased as corpses as opposed to the grand effigies usually sitting above the tombs of nobility.

The Southwark cadaver is the medieval tomb of Thomas Cure, who died in 1588, the same year as the Spanish Armada, during the reign of Elizabeth I. Its skeletal frame is weathered by time, its face disintegrated. It's clearly a dead body, partially wrapped in a shroud, a simple representation of the inevitability of death.

The Canterbury cadaver tomb is on an entirely different scale in terms of grandeur. The tomb of Archbishop Henry Chichele, who died in 1443, has two levels, one showing the effigy of the deceased man in full ecclesiastical robes and, underneath, the cadaver stripped of all its finery, lying naked except for a shroud. It's surrounded by an ornately decorated arch with figures from church history.

A tour guide told me that the archbishop had the tomb built many years before his death so he could look at it every day and contemplate his end.

You can see the pictures at:
www.jfpenn.com/canterburycadavertomb
www.jfpenn.com/southwarkcadavertomb

St Cuthbert's Cave, Northumberland, England

This natural sandstone cave lies within a National Trust reserve on the final day's walk towards Lindisfarne, Holy Island. The cave has a wide mouth and is ringed by a wood of Scots pine. According to legend, the monks fleeing from a medieval Viking invasion stopped in the cave with the remains of St Cuthbert.

It doesn't really matter whether his body lay there or not over a thousand years ago. The cave is clearly a natural shelter from the dark and cold and wild weather, and humans certainly rested and slept here over millennia. There is fire damage and graffiti, both old and new, evidence of people making their mark across time.

On my approach to the cave, an adder with its distinctive zig-zag markings crossed the path in front of me. A protected species, the adder is the UK's only venomous snake, but they are secretive creatures and rarely seen. I had never seen one in the wild before, and it was a precious moment.

As I sat on a rock in the rain eating my lunch, there was a sense of being part of an ancient environment. If I slept in the cave in the dark of night, perhaps I might hear the crackle of ancient flames and the whisper of the long-dead.

You can see a picture at
www.jfpenn.com/stcuthbertscave

Memento mori — Remember, you will die

While walking an ancient route like the Camino de Santiago helps the pilgrim to reflect on mortality, it is almost impossible to comprehend a thousand years of pilgrims walking ahead and many more coming behind.

But while I walked in September 2022, I had a vivid reminder of *memento mori* — remember, you will die — as Queen Elizabeth II died at the age of ninety-six on the second day of my pilgrimage. Snippets of her life punctuated each following day of my Camino on TV in coffee bars and glimpses of newspapers, and I couldn't help but read some of the UK media coverage online when resting at the end of the day.

It was strange to walk outside of my country during such a historically significant week. I remember seeing newly carved statues of the Queen and Prince Philip mounted outside the cathedral in Canterbury on my first pilgrimage in October 2020. The stone was paler than the other sculptures of historic monarchs. The features weren't yet weathered — and of course, both were still alive then. There was a sense of standing next to living history, as another generation passed, and now they are both gone.

I am not an ardent royalist by any means, but the Queen was a constant across my life, as she was for many people in the UK and around the world. As I walked my Camino, the news was full of pictures of her as a young woman, then middle-aged going through the trials of life, then an old woman at her husband's funeral, and in her final days, standing bent over and smiling as she welcomed the new Prime Minister. The span of an extraordinary life against the backdrop of history.

Her life passed by, as will mine and yours. Even a Queen cannot hold back the end.

I walked into Santiago de Compostela on the day of her funeral and, as I rested in my hotel that afternoon, I watched her coffin being lowered into the vault at Windsor Castle. It was a fitting end to my pilgrimage and underscored the sense that something must die for change to happen — new life will emerge from the ashes of the old.

Questions:

- What aspects of history form part of your pilgrimage route?
- Which are you interested in visiting?
- Sometimes it is the unexpected places that mean the most. How can you keep an open mind so serendipity may alight at other times?
- How can 'memento mori' help you put life into perspective?

Resources:

- Pictures of *The History of Old Kent Road* mural by Adam Kossowski
  — www.jfpenn.com/oldkentroadmural
- Pictures of Lesnes Abbey
  — www.jfpenn.com/lesnesabbey
- Pictures of the cadaver tombs
  — www.jfpenn.com/canterburycadavertomb and www.jfpenn.com/southwarkcadavertomb
- Picture of St Cuthbert's Cave
  — www.jfpenn.com/stcuthbertscave

MEMENTO MORI

Remember, you will die.

2.3 A GLIMPSE OF THE DIVINE IN SACRED PLACES

> "All such sites are regarded as thin places, set apart from the world, moving to a different drum, and possessed of an innately special atmosphere because of their connection to another, higher dimension."
>
> —Peter Stanford, *Pilgrimage: Journeys of Meaning*

The paths and final destinations of great pilgrimage routes have been imbued with so much meaning over centuries, they call both to those who believe and those who don't follow a particular faith.

The depth of history and belief of the faithful over generations impart a deeper resonance to certain places where the veil is thin, and you are closer to God, or a sense of the divine. Your pilgrimage will have moments of spiritual meaning if you are open to them, although, of course, they may come at unexpected times.

Here are some moments where I glimpsed the divine while walking these ancient ways.

Crayford Ness, near Dartford, England

I was exhausted as I emerged from the Thames Path Walkway and passed through the gritty, urban sprawl of Erith in East London. I'd already walked around thirty-eight kilometres that day, and I still had several more to walk before I reached my hotel in Dartford. It was October, and dusk was fast approaching.

I took a wrong turn and found myself alongside a busy dual carriageway, the noise of so many cars jolting me back into the modern world. I considered getting a bus or even a taxi to carry me through the last few kilometres, but I had promised myself I would walk every step of my pilgrimage and this was only the first day.

As I trudged on through an industrial estate echoing with the rumble of cranes hauling heavy equipment, the screech of trucks, and the shouts of workers, I wondered what the hell I was doing there.

But then the path opened out onto a flood plain where horses grazed on common land, and the way ahead ran alongside the river once more. This was Erith Saltings, an ancient salt marsh, part of the Thames estuary that can't be built upon as the tide may wash it away. The remains of an ancient fossilised forest dating back to Neolithic times over five thousand years ago lie partially submerged beneath the water, and on the opposite bank lies the Rainham Marshes Nature Reserve. Oyster catchers waded in the shallows, and a regal heron rested on a solitary spar emerging from the water.

But this is no pristine wilderness. The path runs alongside a recycling centre, with the stink of waste coming from huge sorting bins filled with all kinds of discarded human detritus.

I turned my back on the industrial centre and looked out over the salt marsh, as a flock of Canada geese flew overhead, calling to one another in the dusk. With the warbling trill of skylarks and the whistle of the wind off the river, I stood in a moment out of time. The ancient forest buried beneath the waters once echoed with birdsong, and, after human civilisation has passed away, the birds will sing on.

Whether it was the juxtaposition of such ugliness alongside natural beauty, or the timelessness of the fossilised forest with the ephemeral sound of birdsong — or just my exhaustion — I stepped into a thin place there.

After a time, a metallic crash jolted me back to the present. I turned to see an urban fox waiting by the side of the industrial centre, an inquisitive look on his face as I passed by.

My pack seemed lighter as I walked the rest of the way along the River Darent into Dartford, grateful that I had not skipped this part of the journey.

Evensong at Canterbury Cathedral, England

It was dark outside when I entered the cathedral, my final destination on the Pilgrims' Way. With my mask in place, I walked to my solitary chair in the nave, directed by a similarly masked attendant who made sure all present followed pandemic rules. There were a few other people there, all separated by several metres, the space around us cold in the autumn evening.

The choir entered in a line, walking across the nave in robes of purple, all of them masked. They arranged themselves on the steps in front of the quire screen, physically distanced, before removing their face coverings.

They sang psalms in Latin, their voices soaring high into the vault above, harmonising together even as they stood so far apart. This cathedral was built for the glory of God and these men sang for Him too, but also surely for the sheer joy of human voices coming together in song at a time of so much separation.

Ancient stone, ancient words, ancient faith — and the transience of each note disappearing into silence once more.

I stayed for the service, but it was the practice before that truly moved me, and those minutes almost alone in the cathedral nave that freed my spirit. A fitting end to my Pilgrims' Way.

Walking across the sands to Lindisfarne, Holy Island

I rose before the dawn on the final morning of my pilgrimage on the St Cuthbert's Way. I stood at a farm gate looking east into the rising sun, next to a field of curious alpacas and chickens quietly clucking in their roost. As the darkness lifted, the castle on Lindisfarne stood in silhouette against bars of coral clouds, shot through with luminous yellow and pink as the sun rose above the horizon.

The end was so close now.

I was relieved because my muscles ached and I wanted to stop and rest and not walk another day, but I was also sad that the journey was almost over. I wanted to finish the path, but also to keep going. Yet there is nothing beyond Lindisfarne, only the North Sea, and I would reach the furthest point that day.

The clearing sky indicated that the weather would be fine for my crossing of the sands, but I still felt some trepidation. The tidal website warned it was only safe to cross with a guide, and there were tales of walkers lost to the sea in the fog, or cars stranded on the causeway as water reclaimed the land.

But I had prepared, and I knew it was safe to cross. All that remained was to step off onto the sands that the sea left behind.

As the sky turned pale blue, I returned to the farm to retrieve my pack, hefting it onto my shoulders for the last time.

It was only a few kilometres from the farm to the edge of the causeway. I walked with Dave and Keith, pilgrims I had met a few days back after getting lost on the boggy moor. On the way down, Keith and I discovered we had both studied theology and read many of the same books. Whereas I had turned my degree into the basis of my thrillers, he had spent a life of service as a social worker, supporting those with mental health issues. We disagreed on matters of faith, but there was a spark of intellectual connection. Pilgrimage encourages the discussion of such deeper matters and I fleetingly wished we could carry on our debate. But we were soon at the edge of South Low, where the tide had turned and the waters were receding.

Several enormous concrete blocks lay just before the causeway, anti-tank sea defences from World War II. There were signs warning of unexploded ordnance in the area as well as quicksand, and more warnings of what could happen if the tide cut you off. It was hard to imagine the military swarming over this area, now a National Nature Reserve, protected for the biodiversity of life within its shifting sands and tidal waters.

A series of marker poles stretched across the sand to Lindisfarne, interspersed by two wooden refuges on stilts for those who could not beat the tide. The sky was pale blue and clouds scudded high above, and I could see all the way to Holy Island. It was safe to cross.

I rolled my walking trousers up above my knees. Walking barefoot was the traditional way to cross, but I had blisters and raw patches on my feet, so I wore my walking shoes with waterproof socks. I grasped my poles to steady myself — then stepped off the causeway onto the sand.

I wanted to walk the final stretch alone, so after taking photos with Keith and Dave, I let them stride ahead.

The sand was initially firm underfoot as I followed the path of tall wooden poles towards Holy Island. I skirted around deeper pools of water, stepping over the wiggly casts of lugworms and the footprints of wader birds. Gulls flew overhead, their calls piercing the air.

There were patches of grass in places and channels of deeper water to navigate, with sections of sucking mud which I clambered through, using my walking poles to gain a more even footing. I almost lost one shoe in the mud, and it was certainly a more challenging walk than I expected. Less a stroll across firm sand, and more an adventure to reach the final destination.

The lower parts of the wooden guide poles were covered with barnacles and bladder wrack seaweed, surrounded by winkle shells and long strands of sea grass. Crabs scuttled in the shallow water, trying to sink away from the light. The upper parts of the poles that lay above the tide were stark white, reflecting the morning sun, and I could imagine pilgrims spotting them with relief on a foggy crossing.

I stopped halfway across and turned my back on the causeway, looking south across the water to Bamburgh Castle in the distance. A mournful sound pierced the air, a low moan like a chill wind sweeping through ruins. The call of grey seals out on the sand flats, singing as they have for generations of pilgrims. I was just one more in a long line stretching back through history, and my footsteps would wash away with the tide like all who walked here before me.

The crossing took about ninety minutes, with time enough to navigate slowly around the mud and deeper water channels. I finally clambered up the bank on the other side and sat on a bench, looking back at the mainland as I changed into dry shoes.

As with my arrival at Canterbury Cathedral a year ago, there was no fanfare, no one cheering the finish line of my pilgrimage. Only a quiet sense of satisfaction that I had accomplished what I set out to do.

After one last look back at the crossing, I walked into Lindisfarne village. After days of solitude, it was a shock to find hundreds of day-trippers pouring out of coaches and cars, streaming over the causeway while it was open during the narrow tidal window. Throngs of tourists rammed into ice cream shops, artists' studios, and cafes, spilling out into the narrow streets.

While I ate a local crab sandwich in front of the Lindisfarne Mead shop, I wondered what St Cuthbert would have made of the modern Holy Island. There was a frenetic energy about the place as day-trippers rushed to see everything before hurrying back to escape the incoming tide. Some people glanced sideways at me, in a very judgmental English way, as if they didn't appreciate my muddy pack and dishevelled appearance. It was strange to re-enter the real world again.

I hoisted my pack back on and walked to the ruined abbey while it was still open and then visited the parish church of St Mary the Virgin. A full-sized statue of monks carrying the coffin of St Cuthbert stood inside, and I felt more of a connection with those medieval walkers than the modern religious tourists filling the aisles.

As the island emptied, I walked east to Lindisfarne Castle along the shore. Tourists ran in the opposite direction to catch their buses and I was grateful I'd booked a night on the island when it became quiet once more.

I walked until I reached the coast, where cairns of balanced stones stood overlooking the rough waters of the North Sea. The lands beyond were those of Norway and Denmark, and this was the way the Vikings arrived in the eighth century, bringing violence to the abbey and causing the monks to scatter.

I wrote about Lindisfarne in my novella *Day of the Vikings*, a modern-day thriller set against the history of invasion and a supernatural power called down from the ancients. Now finally there in person, I sensed a different power. One that emanated from the island and the power of the tide. There was a part of me that wanted to stay there, to sink into island life, and allow the tide to cut off my access to the wider world.

As I walked back from the castle, a murmuration of starlings swooped above the wetlands. As they soared in unison, forming and reforming different shapes in the twilight, I remembered seeing the same thing at Stonehenge a decade ago. Another place where the veil is thin, a glimpse into a timeless realm where I am just another pilgrim in another sunset.

Questions:

- Where have you experienced this sense of the divine or felt that the veil is thin?
- How can you remain open to the spiritual aspects of pilgrimage without expectation of such moments?
- The end of a journey can be an important time for reflection. How will you mark the end of your pilgrimage?

Resources:

- *Pilgrimage: Journeys of Meaning* — Peter Stanford
- *The Art of Pilgrimage: The Seeker's Guide to Making Travel Sacred* by Phil Cousineau
- Pictures from crossing the sands to Lindisfarne, Holy Island — www.jfpenn.com/crossing
- Canterbury Cathedral — www.booksandtravel.page/canterbury-cathedral

2.4 HARDSHIP AS AN ELEMENT OF PILGRIMAGE

"As for humans, God tests them so they might know they are animals."

—*Ecclesiastes 3:18*

While pain is not a prerequisite for pilgrimage, it's certainly the reality for many. Those sick and suffering, even those on the edge of death, have often traveled on pilgrimage as a petition for healing and a respite from pain. There are even shrines that specialise in certain afflictions.

By journeying to and praying in a specific place, we get a sense of the transactional nature of pilgrimage. As Victoria Preston notes in *We Are Pilgrims*, "If not personal sacrifice, what else can we offer up to the divine in exchange for mercy or redemption?"

PILGRIMAGE

While walking has always helped my mental health and mood, I walked these three pilgrimages in pandemic times and, perhaps for the first time, appreciated how far people might go in the hope of healing.

Jedburgh, Scotland — 5 October 2021

Day 2 of the St Cuthbert's Way

I wake up at two a.m. aware of the pain before I even open my eyes. My whole body aches and I want to sink back into oblivion, but I know these early hours well. I will not sleep again.

It's dark and the sound of rain hammers on the roof outside, as if the storm is trying to get inside and punish me further. The forecast is grim. Heavy rain all day.

Yesterday I walked thirty-five kilometres and I can feel every step. My feet are swollen and bruised, with blisters already forming on my little toes and the side of one big toe. My calves ache from the hills. My hips are puffy and inflamed from carrying my pack. I know it's too heavy, but I can't let anything go. I have bruises on my arms and in weird places on my legs where I must have hit them climbing stiles. My shoulders and my neck ache.

I was so tired last night, I didn't even go out to find food. I thought I would sleep through with so much physical exertion, but I haven't had a good night in a long time, so why would this be any different?

I wake every night soaked in sweat, needing the toilet too many times, worried about money, about what I want to do in life, wanting to escape. I have a recurring nightmare of flying in an old plane with only a glass canopy between me and the sky. As the plane spins upside down, I realise there is no glass and I tumble out into the air, waking with a start as I fall.

I get out of bed, boil the kettle, and make coffee, each step across the floor sending painful sensations through my feet. The tiles are cold in the tiny bathroom, but it helps numb me a little. I take some painkillers with my coffee and eat a flapjack I bought yesterday while I google how to get home from here. There's a bus from Jedburgh back to Berwick-upon-Tweed. I could get the earliest one and then the train and be home before the end of the day.

I email Jonathan at 3.49 a.m.:

Missing you.

I think this might be too much.

I'm still exhausted and in pain.

Can I give up after one day? I just want to come home.

I'm pretty miserable, to be honest.

xxx

I know he will support whatever I choose to do, and the decision is mine to make.

Only I can give up.

Only I can walk on.

The painkillers kick in, dulling the acute sensations, but underneath lies a bone-deep fatigue that I can't seem to shake. I'm almost three months post-COVID and I desperately need to prove to myself that my strength is returning.

I could hardly get out of bed those first few weeks with the virus. I listened to audiobooks about walking so I could move in my mind even as I could not in my body. I couldn't think, let alone work. After those initial weeks, I slowly added back one thing a day, but many afternoons I just had to lie down and rest, crying silently in the dark at how weak I was.

I lost my smell and taste, and I craved texture and salt, eating (too much) crunchy sourdough toast with Bovril (beef spread) to ease the misery. I was depressed and anxious, wondering if I would ever recover. I had never been that sick before, never felt like I wasn't able to do things if I set my mind to them. I always believed that the power of positive thinking could overcome any weakness, and that if I set my mind to a challenge, I could achieve it.

But I am not that person anymore. My flesh is weak, and I am broken.

I am an animal, constrained by my ephemeral, physical body.

I am not a machine. I am not the Terminator.

I can't just keep going and going every day.

Recovery from COVID, or any illness or injury, is not linear. I cannot force it through sheer will.

There was a whisper at the back of my mind as I lay there: What if I never get better?

Below that, a deeper sense of my mortality. Even if I recover, at some point, life *will* be like this again. There will come a time when my body is this weak once more. A time when I will not be able to walk on.

But perhaps today, I can.

In the shower, I press the flesh around my hips.

It's swollen, sensitive, and bruised under the skin and the thought of lifting my pack and tightening the belt once more makes me catch my breath in anticipation of the pain.

I carry too much baggage because I am afraid.

My first aid kit contains everything you could possibly need and more painkillers than a field hospital. I have all kinds of layers of clothing, and two pairs of most things in case one isn't enough. I am carrying a flask for coffee, more provisions than are necessary, and even a paperback book about Northumberland.

I learned my lessons as a Girl Guide: Always be prepared. But I've taken this to extremes in pandemic times. I stocked our cupboards with tins of vegetables and corned beef, hid paracetamol around the house, and stashed extra bottles of water and thick church candles in case the power supply is cut off. Pandemic fear turned me into a prepper, but this need to be prepared is costing me now. I know this, and yet I still cannot leave anything behind.

I drink another two cups of coffee and, although it is only five a.m., I eat an emergency Snickers.

Sugar + painkillers + caffeine = problem solved. At least, for now.

If I can make it through today, then tomorrow I will cross the border from Scotland into England

and I want to make it that far. These borderlands have been fought over for centuries, and the earth is soaked in the blood of those who died for their land. I want to cross the border of my own life — from sick, bedridden, and weak, back into strength. From the darkness of middle-aged ennui back into the light of confidence and creativity and being sure in my direction. If I can make it to Holy Island despite this pain, I will prove to myself that I am on the path to recovery.

As the clock ticks toward six a.m., I pack everything up and dress in full wet weather gear, including waterproof gloves and socks. I hoist my pack onto my bruised hips and let it settle before pulling a bright yellow poncho over everything. I look ridiculous, but this gear is my armour against the storm — both inside and out.

All I have to do is put one foot in front of the other and I will get there.

Pilgrimage is a physical journey

Pilgrimage might be a search for spiritual meaning, but it is also truly a physical experience. Multi-day walks in particular make the pilgrim acutely aware of living in a frail human body. You may struggle for transcendent thought when your feet hurt and you're tired and hungry, too hot or too wet, and your clothes stink of sweat or you're muddy and dirty.

This awareness of the physical self is part of why I find pilgrimage so important. As a writer, I spend most of my time in my head and my body is often an afterthought. But when I get up from my desk after a writing session, I realise how much sedentary life takes its toll.

Unless I am consistent with my workouts, my body is tense and tight when I sit at my computer all day, resulting in headaches; back, neck, and shoulder pain; and a tight right hip that pulls my knee.

While the rigours of a long pilgrimage bring pain, so does daily life. It's just a different kind.

But then how can you be aware of *memento mori* — remember, you will die — if you are not aware of your physical frailty?

Some level of pain and discomfort are to be expected on any pilgrimage

If you undertake a multi-day walk longer than anything you have done before, you are likely to experience some aspect of pain and discomfort along the way. That should not be a surprise!

Maybe it's exhaustion and fatigue, blisters or muscle aches, a twist, sprain, or a fall. It might be an upset stomach, a cold, or headaches. Itchy heat rash, bug bites and stings, chafing from sweaty clothes, or other issues.

There is a difference between low-level pain and acute 'there is definitely something wrong' pain. You need to know how each feels in your body, so you don't over-react or under-react when it occurs.

We experience pain differently depending on our mental state. I don't know whether I was truly in more pain that morning in Jedburgh because of post-COVID fatigue, or whether it really was greater than usual. It didn't matter at the time. I had to overcome it regardless.

If you train for longer distances and walk back-to-back days in preparation, you will get used to the muscular sensation of walking when tired, and potentially with blisters. That will help you understand what a normal level of sensation is and you will also experience recovery over the following days, so you know that pain is short-lived.

How can you reduce your pain?

Physical preparation and training in advance will help develop muscles where you need them for walking.

On the Camino, I met many pilgrims struggling with Achilles tendon problems, twisted knees and ankles, and other leg pain. I didn't have any of this and I can only assume it's because of the amount of walking I do in general, plus my regular weight training.

Look after your feet.

I didn't get blisters or foot issues on the Pilgrims' Way, so I thought I had it all figured out! I know all the tips — make sure your shoes are the right size, change your socks regularly, keep your feet dry, tape sore spots early, use lubricant or hikers' wool. There are so many tips and I've tried most of them, as well as different kinds of socks and blister prevention creams.

Despite everything, I got blisters on both the St Cuthbert's Way and the Camino — due to the combination of wet weather and a too-heavy pack on the former, and long, hot, sweaty days on the latter.

While, clearly, I am not a doctor and this is not medical advice, **carry painkillers** for when you need extra help.

I used normal pharmacy-bought paracetamol and ibuprofen, which you can find in supermarkets and pharmacies along the routes. Please talk to your doctor or pharmacist about your situation before you leave if this is something you're worried about.

Reframe pain as part of the experience, an aspect of the journey that you will overcome and that will make it even more worthwhile.

Pain is temporary. Pride in your accomplishment will remain for the rest of your life.

Consider luggage transfer.

If you carry more weight, you will likely have more pain. If you know in advance that you might struggle, or if you change your mind on the way, there are plenty of companies who will transport your luggage between accommodations on most established pilgrimage routes. You can then walk with a day pack and will certainly suffer less pain. I met many older pilgrims on the Camino, those in their sixties and seventies, who used luggage transfer and they zoomed past me every day!

While my personal 'rules' of pilgrimage included carrying my own bags on these three journeys, I will certainly consider luggage transfer if I do another.

If you need medical help, make sure you can access it

Write down the number of the emergency services if you are traveling to another country. Keep your phone charged so you can call for help if necessary.

Buy appropriate travel insurance, and if you're a UK citizen traveling in Europe, get a Global Health Insurance Card (GHIC) from the NHS that entitles you to healthcare in Europe at local cost.

Questions:

- If you are sick or suffering, how might pilgrimage help you?
- What might you have to adjust to ensure you can finish your pilgrimage?
- How do you cope with pain at the moment?
- How will you cope with pain as part of your pilgrimage?
- How can you prevent excessive pain?
- What will you do if the pain is too much?

Resources:

- *The Art of Pilgrimage: The Seeker's Guide to Making Travel Sacred* — Phil Cousineau
- *The Whole Sole Guide to Walking the Camino de Santiago: How I Walked Over 500 Miles Without Getting a Single Blister or Losing a Toenail* — Maureen Sullivan
- *We Are Pilgrims: Journeys in Search of Ourselves* — Victoria Preston
- Interview with Victoria Preston about We Are Pilgrims — www.booksandtravel.page/secular-pilgrimage/
- List of patron saints of various ailments, accessed 14 November 2022 — en.wikipedia.org/wiki/Patron_saints_of_ailments,_illness,_and_dangers
- UK Global Health Insurance Card — www.nhs.uk/using-the-nhs/healthcare-abroad/apply-for-a-free-uk-global-health-insurance-card-ghic/

2.5 EMBRACE THE PILGRIMAGE INDUSTRY

There is a mythical image of pilgrimage — the solitary pilgrim walks to the top of a hill at sunrise and gazes out across a beautiful landscape as God blesses them with a vision that transforms their life.

There may be such a moment for you, but it is not the reality of most pilgrimage routes — and never has been.

In the gospels, Jesus enters the temple in Jerusalem and drives out "all who were buying and selling there" (Matthew 21:12). Those merchants were serving pilgrims who had journeyed to the temple in Jerusalem for Passover, evidence of pilgrim-related commerce two thousand years ago.

The Canterbury Tales, written between 1387 and 1400 by Geoffrey Chaucer, features a group of pilgrims telling stories on the way to Becket's shrine at Canterbury. It is a contest and the best storyteller wins a free meal at the Tabard Inn at Southwark on return. While the stories are moral tales that illustrate the social, political, and religious concerns of the time, it's clear that the journey has places to stay and food to buy, as well as the option for luxuries on the route.

Commerce has always been an aspect of pilgrimage, and remains so today.

There will be people on the Camino — sometimes lots of them

I'd been thinking about walking the Camino de Santiago for over two decades. I read so many books about it I thought I knew what it would be like. But nothing prepared me for how busy the route would be, even though I walked outside of the main summer season on a quieter route.

The Camino de Santiago has waxed and waned in popularity over the years and now several hundred thousand walk the different routes every year. It is not a wilderness walk, unless you choose the early stages of the Via de la Plata, which are far less developed.

There were moments on the Camino where I was literally, not just metaphorically, part of a long line of pilgrims. Many only walk the last hundred kilometres, so those last few days in particular were really busy.

Aspects of the Camino pilgrim industry

Before you start your pilgrimage, you need to buy the Credential, either at your starting point or online before you go. It is a paper booklet with room for stamps and a QR code for registration, so you can collect your Compostela, the Latin certificate that proves you have finished the Camino.

You must collect stamps along the route from churches and hostels, hotels and restaurants, and this sometimes results in queues in even out-of-the-way places as pilgrims wait for the stamp. On longer routes, you start by getting one stamp per day to prove your journey, and then you need two stamps per day within the last hundred kilometres if walking, and longer if cycling.

> You can see a picture of my Credential with stamps at www.jfpenn.com/credential

In historical times, pilgrims collected a scallop shell when they reached Santiago de Compostela, but these days, pilgrims attach a shell to their pack from the first day. You can buy them in shops along the route, either plain or painted with a cross. I started out by resisting the urge to buy one, but I soon felt a little left out of the pilgrim vibe, so I bought a small, simple scallop shell on the third day and attached it to the back of my pack.

You can see a picture at
www.jfpenn.com/scallopshell

Along the route, there are hotels, B & Bs, and albergues or hostels which exist mainly to cater to pilgrims, as well as cafes and restaurants with pilgrim menus.

Once in Santiago de Compostela, you need to queue at the Pilgrim's Office to have your Credential checked and receive your Compostela.

You can see a picture of mine at
www.jfpenn.com/compostela

You can also buy a Certificate of Distance as proof of the exact number of kilometres travelled.

The Pilgrim's Office has many souvenirs and the shops surrounding the cathedral also sell every kind of pilgrim merchandise you could possibly desire. The same is true at Canterbury and Lindisfarne.

Here's me in my 'pilgrim' T-shirt at Canterbury in October 2020: www.jfpenn.com/pilgrimtshirt

The Pilgrims' Mass is held three times a day at the Cathedral of Santiago de Compostela and they read out the countries of the pilgrims who arrived that day. Over 1,500 pilgrims arrived in the city on the day I walked in. The Camino is certainly not a solitary route.

Your attitude to the pilgrimage industry will shape your experience on the Camino

There are two possible attitudes to this industry.

You can resent the intrusion of so many people and the overt commercialism, and pine for a solo, spiritual pilgrimage — or you can embrace it and join in wholeheartedly.

After some initial reluctance, I did the latter and enjoyed supporting the local businesses that play an important part in the Camino experience. I appreciated the comfortable accommodation, pharmacies and supermarkets, as well as coffee shops, restaurants, and bars along the Way. I also stopped in some sections to let waves of chattering pilgrims pass, and I relished moments of quiet walking when

I didn't see another person for a while, mainly when I left before sunrise on a few mornings.

My favourite day's walk was Baiona to Vigo, or at least the first twenty kilometres of it. The main Camino route went through the hills, but there was a slightly longer alternate route following the coast north. I chose the coastal route, which was barely way-marked, but by keeping the sea on my left, it was easy enough to navigate along paths and boardwalks.

I left Baiona in the dark and walked north as dawn broke over the coastal wetlands. Wading birds picked their way through the shallows and finches darted between bushes on the shore. The path followed alongside almost deserted beaches, with just a few dog walkers on the sand. It was a cool autumnal weekday morning. There were heavy clouds overhead, and the wind blew rain in later that day. I mostly walked alone, happy to have taken the alternative route, to step out of the stream of pilgrims even just for a day.

If you want a quieter pilgrimage, adjust your route or time of year

The Camino would certainly be quieter off season, in the late autumn or winter, but many of the accommodation and food options would be closed and your experience would be harder in different ways.

You could also choose a different pilgrimage altogether, since while the Camino is busy, many others are relatively empty. The Pilgrims' Way was quiet, but then I walked it in the early days of the pandemic, so I would expect it to be busier in 'normal' times.

I walked most of the St Cuthbert's Way alone, sometimes for hours with no one else in sight. While it is not a 'wilderness' walk and there is accommodation each night and places to buy food, it is certainly more solitary and not a popular trail like the Camino. In terms of that mythical pilgrimage experience, I found glimpses of it on the St Cuthbert's Way, for sure.

Questions:

- What are the pros and cons of the pilgrimage industry? How might it affect your pilgrimage?
- How can you embrace the industry — or avoid it completely?

Resources:

- Credential with stamps — www.jfpenn.com/credential
- Scallop shell on backpack — www.jfpenn.com/scallopshell
- Compostela certificate — www.jfpenn.com/compostela
- Jo Frances Penn in 'pilgrim' T-shirt at Canterbury, October 2020 — www.jfpenn.com/pilgrimtshirt

2.6 EATING ON PILGRIMAGE

I love food, and like many people, I have a complicated relationship with it. But pilgrimage is not a time to be precious about food, mainly because you don't get a lot of choice most of the time.

Most pilgrimage routes are well supported with places to buy basic food

If you're worried about finding food each day, don't worry. A pilgrimage is not a wilderness walk and there are plenty of places to buy food, if not during the day, then at the stopping places each night — hotels, bars, hostels, supermarkets, local shops, even vending machines.

Pilgrimage is not about gastronomy

Most of the food options are pretty basic and repetitive, especially if you're on a budget, but if you get a chance to sample local specialities, then embrace it as part of your experience.

Before walking the St Cuthbert's Way, I spent the night in Berwick-upon-Tweed on the border between England and Scotland. I had the best fish stew of my life that night at the Queen's Head pub, made from freshly caught fish and seafood.

At A Guarda in Spain, after crossing the river from Portugal, I had a memorable plate of fresh scallops cooked in butter and a half bottle of local Albariño.

As a solo traveler, restaurants can often find you a seat as a walk-in, so take advantage if you have the budget and the opportunity.

Give up, or at least relax, your usual eating routine

In my normal daily life, I follow intermittent fasting, and usually only eat after midday. On the Camino, the accommodation usually provides breakfast and, since it's already paid for, most pilgrims eat it. Some places even let you take an extra roll or piece of fruit with you.

I changed my eating pattern to include breakfast and generally skipped an evening meal, especially in Portugal and Spain, where restaurants open much later and I was ready for bed most nights at the time I would have been sitting down to eat.

I found supermarkets to buy lunch and ate a smaller snack in the early evening rather than a full dinner. I took a plastic spork (spoon-fork combo) which was handy for eating in my room.

If you have particular dietary requirements, you may struggle in some of the smaller places, so bring back-up protein bars or, if possible, bend your normal rules while you're away.

Pilgrimage is not about weight loss

That may sound ridiculous to those who don't consider such things, but I met several people who were trying to get fit and lose weight on the Camino. Personally, I came back from Spain several kilos *heavier* even after walking 300 kilometres, mainly because the staple food is delicious local bread, served with everything at every meal and the cheapest option available if you are on a budget.

Food is fuel

Make sure you carry enough food for the day and check the route for somewhere to buy a meal or stock up. The St Cuthbert's Way has some remote walking, where there was nowhere to buy coffee or food once I was on my way.

I was grateful for my flask of coffee on cold days and stopped in pubs or bars for coffee and pastries, soup, or whatever was on offer when I could on each route.

At the end of a long, hot day on the Camino on the outskirts of Padrón, I stopped in a bar for a cold beer. There were a few locals sitting watching sport and since I was off the main pilgrim track, they considered me a curiosity with my pack and red face from walking in the sun. I ordered an Estrella Galicia beer, and the barman brought me a little bowl of hot chickpeas with a chunk of chorizo sausage to go with it. I would not have ordered such a dish, but at that moment, it was everything I needed. Salty and delicious. It fuelled me for the last push out to the rural hotel.

Food is emotional support

When I am exhausted and broken and hurting, food helps. Specifically Snickers bars, which I rarely eat outside of walking expeditions. There's just something satisfying about them when I need a pick-me-up.

I also love my coffee. On the St Cuthbert's Way and the Pilgrims' Way, I carried a flask and made it with instant coffee every morning. UK accommodation will usually provide a kettle, whereas in Europe (and the USA) it is not so common.

On the Camino, I fuelled up with coffee at breakfast and then stopped for espresso along the way whenever I could. At least in Portugal, I could usually find a cup for under a euro.

Alcohol (in moderation) can be a wonderful thing

Some choose a sober pilgrimage for short-term abstinence or part of a bigger life decision.

Personally, I enjoy a drink as part of relaxation in the evening and also to sample local beverages. The Camino route out of Porto gives you access to some of the best local wine in the world from both Portugal and Spain, and a cold Estrella Galicia beer after walking twenty kilometres on a hot day with another ten to go can help speed you along the path.

Lindisfarne, Holy Island, at the end of the St Cuthbert's Way has its own mead made from local honey as well as gin from botanicals. Well worth a try!

Questions:

- What are your expectations of food on pilgrimage? How might it affect your trip positively or negatively?

- How can you leave behind some of your usual food-related behaviours and embrace the difference on your pilgrimage?

- Is there any essential food or drink you want to bring with you or determine the availability of along your route? Or are you happy to leave it to serendipity?

2.7 FACING THE CHALLENGE

"A journey without challenge has no meaning; one without purpose has no soul."

—Phil Cousineau, *The Art of Pilgrimage*

I woke up on the eighth day of my Camino in the village of Oia, Spain. A hurricane had blown through the night before, cutting power to the area as I lay in bed listening to the violence of the storm. It was still dark and rain pounded down outside.

As I taped my feet and plastered my blisters, I wondered what the hell I was doing. I did not want to walk out into the storm, especially when every step was painful. I still had seven more days of walking to get to Santiago de Compostela, and given the state of my feet, it would only get harder.

But pilgrimage is not a holiday.

It is meant to be a challenge — and part of the challenge is not giving up.

A long-distance walk is a test of stamina. Each day might be manageable and nothing too challenging if it were the only one, but repeating the challenge day after day — especially on the cobblestones of the Portuguese route — compounds the fatigue and pain.

Practically, it's easy to give up on the Camino, as you can call a taxi at most accommodations and other places along the route each day. Many pilgrims choose to skip a stage and take transport to their next hotel, so the temptation is always there — and if you truly need help, then, of course, you must take it.

But I know the difference between the 'normal' pain of long-distance walking and acute 'something is definitely wrong' pain.

At times like these, when the struggle is more mental than physical, I write in my journal. Some might pray, but I find solace and answers in writing.

I moan a lot and list all the places that hurt and why I want to stop and give up and go home. Then I write about why I am walking and why I should continue. I know this pain is temporary and it will fade, but the pride in finishing will be mine for the rest of my life.

I write my affirmations over and over again: I am strong. I can do hard things. I will finish.

That morning in Oia, I drank my coffee, put on my rain gear, and headed out into the storm.

Pilgrimage proves you can do difficult things, and that knowledge will help you when you return to your daily life. If you can figure out the challenges along the way, be resilient, and make it to your destination, you prove your strength to yourself. I needed that at a time of turmoil in my life when, most days, I felt weak and broken in so many ways.

There are three stages of pilgrimage that require different aspects of determination.

Starting energy

You need starting energy to plan and organise your trip, to turn it from a long-held dream or a goal into reality. You need to overcome obstacles and fears to get even as far as the starting point, and many people fall at this first hurdle.

You need to book time away from your normal life and, since most of the Camino routes are a physical challenge, you also need to train in preparation, which takes more time.

I'd been wanting to walk the Camino for more than twenty years, and I only found my starting energy when the pandemic put the brevity of life into perspective. I know how it feels to say 'some day,' but that day will never come unless you make a decision, book a route and transport to get there, and commit to your pilgrimage.

Pushing-through energy

Once you begin your pilgrimage, you need pushing-through energy, especially on the days when you're tired and in pain and emotionally broken and you just want to give up, like that morning in Oia for me.

You will need it when the weather is wild and stormy, or too hot and the sun beats down upon you. You will need it when your feet hurt and your pack is too heavy and there are still days to go until you finish. You will need it when you are bored with the monotony of seemingly endless walking. You will need it when you get annoyed with other pilgrims, and when you wonder why you are bothering to do this, anyway.

You will need this pushing-through energy in so many situations, but somehow you will keep putting one foot after the next until that final step when you arrive at your destination.

Finishing energy

You need finishing energy to return home and reflect on the experience, to bring the lessons of pilgrimage to the rest of your life.

It's easy to arrive home, put your pack away and your clothes in the wash, then dive back into the inevitable life admin and everything you've missed.

By the time your blisters have healed, you may have already forgotten the lessons of the Way, and finishing energy is needed to find the gold and incorporate it into your life.

It might be re-reading your journal, or going through your photos and printing those that resonate. It might be taking action on a decision you made on your walk.

Don't just slip back into life as if nothing has changed. The gifts of pilgrimage take time to emerge, so allow space for them to filter through.

Questions:

- Do you have starting energy? If not, how can you find it?
- Are you ready to commit to your pilgrimage?
- How will you develop pushing-through energy? Are there ways you can start practicing it in your daily life?
- If you are planning your pilgrimage, how can you make space for finishing energy on your return?

Resources:

- *The Art of Pilgrimage: The Seeker's Guide to Making Travel Sacred* — Phil Cousineau

"IT IS YOUR PILGRIMAGE *and as in life, you must walk it your way.*"

J.F. PENN

2.8 PILGRIMAGE IN A CHANGING SEASON

"Something in me is changing season."
—Raynor Winn, *The Salt Path*

I walked my three pilgrimages in the northern hemisphere autumn as the seasons changed. The leaves turned brown and dropped from the branches. There was a chill in the wind's edge. I could see the beginning of winter ahead.

I didn't know it at the time, but these walks reflected my own changing season, as my body and mind shifted into a new phase of life.

17 July 2020

I haven't slept properly since last November so it's not just the pandemic. Most nights I wake around two a.m. — sometimes it's hot sweats, then cold chills, and sometimes it's just my mind in overdrive.

Everything feels pointless. Some days I don't care about anything at all. I just want to stay in bed all day. There is no feeling, no up, no down. I am a blank.

Jonathan said yesterday that I seem sad all the time and it's true, there is very little that brings me joy at the moment. Work is monotonous. I am tired all the time. I don't have the creative energy to write.

I've tried black cohosh, valerian, CBD oil, and other herbal remedies. I reduced my caffeine. I tried meditating. I sleep on the couch most nights so Jonathan can get a full night's sleep without me disturbing him by constantly getting up. It's a circle of night sweats, going to the toilet, drinking water as my mouth is so dry, getting chills, huddling back under the covers, and then the cycle repeats, sometimes several times a night.

There are waves of emotion and I cry for no reason. I'm not someone who cries like this, but some days I just can't stop.

This is not like me. I have always been a default

happy soul, but I don't recognise that person anymore. I can still channel her positivity in public — fake it 'til you make it — and that helps me through. At least briefly, I remember how I used to be.

It's an animal thing. I have no control over it. Days of bleeding followed by days of misery, a feeling of getting old, and the loss of a significant part of myself.

The wave sweeps over me and some days, I can ride it and others I am left spluttering in its wake. If I open my mouth, I could let the water rush in and then it would all be over.

But I guess I can make it through another day.

As long as I don't run away from it all, as long as I don't burn it all down, then I can get through this.

Thoughts of transience and permanence

What passes? What remains?

These questions kept coming up for me as I walked my pilgrimages, and remain with me still as I read the words from my journal above. So many transient emotions that some days I don't even recognise as my own, and yet, I still remain.

The transience of the natural world was in

evidence as I walked each autumn, particularly on my UK pilgrimages. Golden light on the leaves falling from chestnut trees. Beech nuts and acorns on the muddy path ahead. The last of the blackberries in the hedgerows, with rose-hips and elderberries growing nearby. Wild rabbits running through the fields and pheasants startled from the bushes. The cry of a kite in the cloudy sky above.

The death of another season as the world turns once more. The cold bite of the winter wind and the hope of spring ahead.

How many more turnings do I have left?

Pilgrimage teaches that the way can change according to fleeting emotion. Sometimes the map looked huge, the distances enormous. My will was diminished and my body was weak. I felt bruised and broken and ugly.

At other times, the kilometres disappeared swiftly under my feet, my spirit soared, and I walked with a smile on my face. My body was strong and well and beautiful.

At times, my feelings distorted the path, and at others, the way changed me. My pain and my emotions were transient. I could only capture them in writing each day, before they passed into memory.

The experience of pilgrimage itself is transient, but the lessons learned — and my pride in the accomplishment — are etched permanently on my heart.

NOTE: I am not a doctor and this is not medical advice. It is just my opinion based on experience. Please see a medical professional for your situation.

Update November 2022:

I stopped sleeping properly in November 2019, before the pandemic, but later blamed my insomnia on anxiety about COVID-19. It certainly didn't help! I tried all kinds of remedies and therapies but nothing worked. By April 2022, I couldn't deal with the lack of sleep anymore. I spent my days teetering on the edge of coping, and I had to do something to fix it.

I spoke to a menopause doctor and went on hormone replacement therapy (HRT). Within forty-eight hours of applying an oestrogen patch, I slept for a full night and have done so since. Tears well up as I write this, because it was truly a miracle.

My hot flushes and night sweats went away, my misery lifted, and I began to feel like myself again. I still wake in the night, but in a normal way, and I go back to sleep almost immediately. I can sleep in the same bed as Jonathan and no longer have night after night awake on the couch.

Of course, HRT is not for everyone, but at this point in my life, it helped immeasurably. Suicide rates for women are highest in the menopausal age bracket (forty-five to fifty-four) and I certainly felt a draw to it before HRT. Part of me did not want to mention such a topic within a travel memoir, but it has been such a significant part of my personal life in the last few years, I want to share the information in case it helps someone else.

If you or anyone you love is going through this time of life, I recommend *Menopausing: The Positive Roadmap to Your Second Spring* by Davina McCall, co-written with a medical doctor. It goes into detail on the many varied symptoms, as well as the evidence behind modern HRT.

Questions:

- What season of your life are you in?
- What part might pilgrimage play in the transition between the seasons of life and your acceptance of it?

Resources:

- *The Salt Path* — Raynor Winn
- *Menopausing: The Positive Roadmap to Your Second Spring* — Davina McCall

PART 3: ARRIVING AND THE RETURN

3.1 ARRIVING ON A PILGRIMAGE

"Allow time for your soul to catch up."

—Phil Cousineau, *The Art of Pilgrimage*

There comes a moment on every pilgrimage when you see your destination ahead and you realise your journey is almost over.

There's a sense of relief, especially if your last day has been a long, hard walk, and you are looking forward to a shower and a rest. But there's also sadness as your pilgrimage is ending. Tomorrow you will not rise and walk into the dawn once more. Tomorrow, you will be back in the real world.

While the crossing to Lindisfarne, Holy Island, was far more than I expected and a fitting end to a pilgrimage, my arrival for the Pilgrims' Way and the Camino were anticlimactic, even disappointing. But they are just as important to share.

There is no fanfare

I arrived at Canterbury Cathedral Lodge at the end of the Pilgrims' Way an hour before Evensong. There was no fanfare, no choir of angels, no crowd of supporters cheering me on as I crossed the finish line on my first solo multi-day walk, my first pilgrimage. No one even gave me a second glance.

It had rained all day, and I was still wearing all my wet weather gear as I checked in. The young woman on the front desk asked where I had walked from.

"London," I said, a note of pride in my voice.

"Oh, what time did you set off this morning?" she replied.

In these days of cars and trains, she had no sense of how many days' walk it took to get between the cities and no idea of the six days I'd spent on foot. For a moment, I was disappointed that she didn't appreciate the effort it had taken for me to get there, but pilgrimage is not for others to appreciate. It is only for the pilgrim to know what the journey means and how much effort it takes. I had more of a chance to reflect on the journey when I attended Evensong, as I described in chapter 2.3, but that immediate arrival experience was deflating rather than inspiring.

The moment of arrival may not be what you expect

There are truths you don't really appreciate until you live them. These pilgrimages taught me that it really is about the journey and not the destination.

As satisfying as it is to arrive at the end of a pilgrimage, it is not the final place that changes you, but every step along the way.

Before my Camino, I spent decades imagining walking into the city of Santiago de Compostela. During the dark days of the early pandemic, the thought of carrying my pack into the Praza do Obradoiro in front of the cathedral sustained me.

But to get to that square, you have to walk through the suburbs of what is a busy Spanish city. My first glimpse of the cathedral was from a motorway underpass, and it was a shock to walk through the busy streets on the way ahead. In those final kilometres, I lost the way-markers and ended up using Google Maps to navigate the bustling shopping streets.

I had imagined an open boulevard leading to the square and the occasional pilgrim walking in quiet contemplation — but the warren of narrow streets was disorienting and packed full of tourists. I was buffeted from every direction as I strained to see the cathedral ahead.

When I finally reached the square, it was with more of a sense of relief than triumph. It was also a very hot day and my obligatory selfie in front of the cathedral was red-faced and gasping. The pain in my feet intensified, as if my body had given up on arrival, and my fatigue was bone deep.

I had imagined sitting at a cafe on that square, drinking a cold beer as I watched other pilgrims arrive with joyful footsteps. But there are no cafes on Praza do Obradoiro, and actually, I just wanted a shower and some food and a rest. I stayed in the square only minutes before walking on to my hotel, and there was a dull sense of emptiness instead of triumph in my halting, painful gait.

Allow an extra day or two at the destination

Each of my pilgrimages ended at a historic place, and I stayed an extra night or two at each one so I could experience them with fresh eyes after the end of my journey.

You might arrive late in the day as I did into Canterbury, with little time to see anything. On Lindisfarne, the tides circumscribe when sites are open on the island and once you've walked across, there is little time left to see anything. I did a quick walk around the ruined abbey and church before they closed for the day and was even ushered out of the bookshop as the proprietor rushed to get over the causeway before the waters covered it once more.

You might also arrive tired and in pain, as I did in Santiago de Compostela, with no energy to appreciate the place.

But you will wake the next morning with a fresh perspective and no need to pull on your pack or lace up your boots once more. That's when you can let your accomplishment sink in and see the place of significance you have journeyed to.

After my Camino, I woke early in Santiago de Compostela and walked to the Pilgrim's Office to get my Compostela. It was cold and windy that morning as I queued with other pilgrims, but it was worth the wait.

My Compostela certificate was proof that I had walked the requisite distance along the Camino. It was tangible evidence of effort and even though I still hobbled along with plasters on my feet, I couldn't help but smile with pride.

I went to the Pilgrims' Mass that morning and also visited the cathedral separately to wander around and take pictures. I indulged in churros (fried doughnut sticks) and hot chocolate for breakfast, and later, I toasted myself with a cold

PILGRIMAGE

glass of Albariño and some local seafood. The day after I walked into that square, I finally felt I had arrived and finished my pilgrimage.

> "All journeys have secret destinations
> of which the traveler is unaware."
> —Martin Buber

Questions:

- What are your expectations of arriving on the final day of your pilgrimage? Can you release those expectations and just let it be whatever it is?
- How can you "allow time for your soul to catch up," as Phil Cousineau puts it?

Resources:

- *Pilgrimage: The Seeker's Guide to Making Travel Sacred* — Phil Cousineau
- My pictures from the Cathedral of Santiago de Compostela on the day after arrival — www.booksandtravel.page/santiago-de-compostela-cathedral/
- My pictures from Lindisfarne at the end of the Pilgrims' Way — www.booksandtravel.page/st-cuthberts-way-lindisfarne/
- My pictures from Canterbury Cathedral — www.booksandtravel.page/canterbury-cathedral/

3.2 RETURNING HOME

"Before enlightenment; chop wood, carry water. After enlightenment; chop wood, carry water."

—Zen Buddhist proverb

Returning home is part of pilgrimage. It is not meant to be long-term travel or exploration for no purpose. It is a journey of meaning to a specific destination, and once you have completed it, you must return home.

You might be welcomed back with a hug from a partner or friend, or a cuddle from enthusiastic pets, but the celebration will be brief and normal life will resume once more. You will put your dirty clothes in the wash and cook your favourite dinner and settle back to catch up on the TV you missed. You'll do the inevitable life admin that piled up while you were away. You'll go back to work and return to the routines of home.

There will be moments when you appreciate the simple pleasures you took for granted before leaving, but soon, they will become part of normal life again. Your pilgrimage will fade into memory.

The gifts of pilgrimage take time to emerge

The myth of walking pilgrimage entices people into thinking that it will enable some great life transformation. That a moment of divine inspiration will strike and the pilgrim will return changed forever.

That might happen, but equally there may be no transformational pivot point — and that's okay. It may take time to well up, or it may not come at all. The expectation of such a change may prevent you from seeing smaller shifts, so try to stay open to possibility.

Take time to process your journey, whatever that means to you, and if you find no gifts, no gold, then perhaps you haven't finished your pilgrimage journey yet.

My three pilgrimages of meaning

I always intended to write a pilgrimage book, and I had thought I would write it after the Pilgrims'

Way. For some reason, I expected a six-day walk to miraculously cure me of midlife ennui and pandemic locked-in-locked-down misery.

The walk was a much-needed escape, and I had moments of joy on the way, but no real clarity emerged. I had expected to find answers and write deep and meaningful insights in my journal, but it was filled with the practicalities of walking, glimpses of the physical landscape, and disjointed fragments of emotion.

Soon after I returned from that first pilgrimage in November 2020, the UK went back into another lockdown, followed by an even longer one in early 2021. It was a hard winter, so I planned my next escape, buying the St Cuthbert's Way guidebook and maps of the route, fully expecting to walk it at full strength when the world had recovered from COVID-19, which we all expected to happen quickly.

But of course, it didn't.

Bath, England — 6 February 2021

I walked alone in the freezing fog this morning, then lay weeping on the sofa. I am not okay. I feel like one of those caged animals who pace back and forth, wearing down the same paths, desperate to get out. I want something to happen, anything. No one is even zooming anymore. There is nothing to say. We're all done.

I caught the virus in July 2021 and I was the sickest I've ever been. When I walked the St Cuthbert's Way in the following October, it was partly to prove I was on the path to recovery, a short-term goal that I achieved — and yet the world had still not recovered.

Soon after my return from that pilgrimage in November 2021, we flew to New Zealand to visit my mother-in-law, the first time Jonathan could see her for almost two years. As New Zealand citizens, we were allowed into the country, but we spent a week locked in a hotel room and further days in isolation before we emerged into a fear-ridden Auckland.

Trapped in that hotel room, guarded by the military with only half an hour per day permitted outside walking in a circle around a parking lot, I sunk back into darkness. Jonathan gave me his time slot on several days, just so I could be outside. My tattered wings bled from bashing desperately against the bars of my cage once more.

New Zealand had just emerged from lockdown and the virus had yet to arrive. Fear was heightened and the bureaucracy of international vaccination certificates kept us from even buying a takeaway coffee. Any glimpse of freedom I had gained on the St Cuthbert's Way was buried under the weight of renewed pandemic constraints.

By the time I walked the Camino de Santiago in September 2022, pandemic restrictions were almost completely gone in the UK and Europe. I wore a mask on the plane and on public transport, but outside on the Camino, it was as if there was no virus. You could smile at another pilgrim and see their smile in response.

My freedom to roam was restored once more, and I began to find meaning in my personal chaos.

As I returned from my Camino, I realised that home was where I wanted to be — back in Bath, with Jonathan.

I've always struggled with the idea of home, more interested in visiting new places and moving on, starting afresh. I didn't understand the attraction of putting down roots or settling in one place, preferring the reinvention of a new city, a new country, a new culture.

In my teenage years, I was in love with Bruce

Chatwin — or at least the idea of him as he died in 1989 before I even heard his name. I read all his books and wrote my journal in Moleskine notebooks because he had used them. I went to Australia because of his book *The Songlines*, and his words summed up my desire to move.

"Man's real home is not a house, but the road, and life itself is a journey to be walked on foot."

Bruce Chatwin was forty-eight when he died. His illness forced him to stop wandering, and his restlessness was stilled by the grave.

I am almost forty-eight as I write this, and these three pilgrimages over the last two years have calmed my wanderlust. The restrictions of the pandemic lockdowns made me walk the same local paths over and over as the seasons changed, and in the process, I put down roots and discovered what home might be.

A few weeks after I returned from the Camino, we adopted two British Shorthair cats, Cashew and Noisette. As I write this, Cashew lies next to me in a sunbeam by the window, purring quietly, while Jonathan works upstairs in his loft, Noisette on the beanbag beside him.

Pilgrimage teaches the blessing of simple pleasures, and gratitude for another precious day on this earth. I will walk alone again, but for now, I am home and that is enough.

> "When I let go of who I am,
> I become who I might be."
>
> —Lao Tzu

Questions:

- How will you make time for your return to normal life?
- How will you reflect and learn from your experience?
- How can you allow time and space for the gifts of pilgrimage to emerge?

Resources:

- *The Songlines* — Bruce Chatwin
- *What Am I Doing Here?* — Bruce Chatwin

WHEN I LET GO OF WHO I AM,

I become who I might be.

LAO TZU

CONCLUSION: THE END IS THE BEGINNING

> "Not I, not anyone else, can travel that road for you. You must travel it for yourself."
>
> —Walt Whitman, *Song of Myself*

Many people walk pilgrimage at a time of change — out of a need to reset, find a new direction in life, recover from grief, or find an answer to a question.

These three pilgrimage routes together over the last two years have certainly been a path of change through a rocky period in my life, and in the world in general. My solo pilgrimages helped calm my anger, frustration, and grief at everything going on in the world and my inability to change it. They have given me much during difficult times.

When I started my pilgrimage journey in October

2020, the pandemic still raged and I was stuck in the anger stage of grief, with a side of depression. I walked myself into submission over that time.

The St Cuthbert's Way helped me prove to myself that I had the strength to carry on even while still suffering from post-COVID fatigue, and I found solace in the natural beauty of Northumberland.

When I walked the Camino de Santiago in September 2022, the world had moved on, and in many ways, so had I. The Way was not a catalyst for change but a culmination and celebration of two years of shifting perspective.

It's the end of one season and the beginning of another. Perhaps that's just one gift of middle age, but regardless, walking the Camino was the completion of a life goal and it closed one chapter so I can begin another.

There is a small stone marker outside Canterbury Cathedral, speckled with lichen. Most people walk straight past without even noticing it's there. It depicts a pilgrim striding onward with his staff and bag, and marks the beginning of the Via Francigena, which runs from Canterbury to Rome. The route covers 1,700 kilometres and requires a few months to walk its length.

When I left Canterbury that final morning after the Pilgrims' Way, I stood at that stone with my pack on my back. For a moment, I considered walking on and surrendering to the call of the way once more.

Then I turned my back on it and headed home.

I would set out on another pilgrimage — but not today.

EPILOGUE

It's an early autumn morning, and a chill wind blows along the river Avon. Leaves in shades of rust spin from bare branches and spiral into the rushing waters beneath.

A squirrel darts along a branch carrying an acorn as a swan glides along beneath. Late-flowering cyclamen with petals of mauve peek through the carpet of dead leaves. A glimmer of new life as the year turns once more.

Jonathan wraps his arms around me as we stand on the bridge together looking out over the water. As the river flows past, we walk on, hand in hand.

ENJOYED PILGRIMAGE?

If you loved the book and have a moment to spare, I would really appreciate a short review.

Your help in spreading the word is gratefully appreciated and reviews make a huge difference to helping new readers find my books. Thank you!

Join my fiction Reader's Group and get a free thriller ebook

You'll also be notified of new releases, giveaways and receive personal updates from behind the scenes of my thrillers and photos from my research trips. Sign up at:

www.JFPenn.com/free

Books and Travel Podcast

Interviews and solo episodes about the deeper side of books and travel.

Available on your favourite podcast app. Find the backlist episodes at:

www.BooksAndTravel.page/listen

For writers:
Sign up for my free Author Blueprint

If you need help with writing fiction or non-fiction, publishing, book marketing, or making a living with your writing, you'll find lots of useful information at:

www.TheCreativePenn.com/blueprint

For writers: The Creative Penn Podcast

Join me every Monday at The Creative Penn Podcast where I talk about writing, publishing, book marketing and the author business.

Available on your favourite podcast app. Find the backlist episodes at:

www.TheCreativePenn.com/podcast

ABOUT J.F. PENN

J.F. Penn is the Award-nominated, New York Times and USA Today bestselling author of the ARKANE action adventure thrillers, Brooke & Daniel psychological/crime thrillers, and the Mapwalker fantasy adventure series, as well as other standalone stories.

Her books weave together ancient artifacts, relics of power, international locations, and adventure with an edge of the supernatural. Joanna lives in Bath, England and enjoys a nice G&T.

www.JFPenn.com
joanna@JFPenn.com
www.Facebook.com/JFPennAuthor
www.Instagram.com/JFPennAuthor
www.BooksAndTravel.page

For writers:

Joanna's site, www.TheCreativePenn.com empowers authors with the knowledge they need to choose their creative future. Books and courses by Joanna Penn, as well as her award-winning show, *The Creative Penn Podcast*, provide information and inspiration on how to write, publish and market books, and make a living as a writer.

BOOKS BY J.F. PENN / JOANNA PENN

You can find all my books at www.CreativePennBooks.com and also on your favourite online bookstore in all the usual formats.

ARKANE Action-Adventure Thrillers

Stone of Fire #1
Crypt of Bone #2
Ark of Blood #3
One Day In Budapest #4
Day of the Vikings #5
Gates of Hell #6
One Day in New York #7
Destroyer of Worlds #8
End of Days #9
Valley of Dry Bones #10
Tree of Life #11
Tomb of Relics #12
Short story: Soldiers of God

Brooke and Daniel Psychological/Crime Thrillers

Desecration #1
Delirium #2
Deviance #3

Mapwalker Dark Fantasy Adventures

Map of Shadows #1
Map of Plagues #2
Map of the Impossible #3

Short Stories

A Thousand Fiendish Angels
The Dark Queen
Blood, Sweat, and Flame

Other Books

Risen Gods — co-written with J. Thorn

American Demon Hunters: Sacrifice — co-written with J. Thorn, Lindsay Buroker, and Zach Bohannon

Non-Fiction Books As Joanna Penn

How to Write Non-Fiction

How to Market a Book

How to Make a Living with your Writing

Productivity for Authors

Successful Self-Publishing

Your Author Business Plan

The Successful Author Mindset

The Relaxed Author

Public Speaking for Authors, Creatives and Other Introverts

Audio for Authors: Audiobooks, Podcasting, and Voice Technologies

The Healthy Writer

Business for Authors

Co-writing a Book

Career Change

Artificial Intelligence, Blockchain, and Virtual Worlds

www.TheCreativePenn.com/books

APPENDICES, WORKBOOK, AND OTHER RESOURCES

You can find the appendices with links to more resources and downloadable extras at www.jfpenn.com/pilgrimagedownload

There is also a Companion Workbook with all the questions from the book, which you can download as a PDF edition or buy in print at: www.jfpenn.com/pilgrimageworkbook

APPENDIX 1: QUESTIONS BY CHAPTER

You can download this list at
www.jfpenn.com/pilgrimagedownload

Why pilgrimage?

- Why are you interested in pilgrimage rather than another kind of journey?

- What might pilgrimage give you? Why do you need that?

- Do you feel called to a particular pilgrimage? Why is that?

A personal faith

- Is pilgrimage a matter of faith for you?
- If yes, how can you incorporate your belief into your preparations in order to make the pilgrimage even better?
- If no, are there ways you can open yourself up to the possibility of spiritual moments along the way?

Part 1: Preparation

1.1 Which pilgrimage?

- Do you feel called to a particular pilgrimage?
- What pilgrimages are available in your country?
- How far do you want to walk and for how many days?
- How comfortable are you with multi-day walking? How could you work up to it?
- Do you want to walk solo, or with someone else or in a group? Are you drawn to a more popular route or one that's more isolated?
- Do you want to know where you're sleeping each night or are you happy to go free range?

- Do you want to carry your pack or get luggage transfer?
- How will these choices affect your budget?
- Are you walking your own path in life? Are you living by other people's definition of success? How can you walk your own path once more?
- What do you want to achieve on your pilgrimage? How will you keep your personal definition of success in mind during your journey?

1.2 Walking alone or with others

- How do you feel about the prospect of walking solo?
- How do you feel about walking in a group?
- How can you use those feelings to help you make decisions about your pilgrimage?
- How can you walk 'your pilgrimage, your way'?
- How can you tap into what you truly love, rather than relying on the opinions of others?
- How is solitude a part of your life? Does it recharge you? How could you incorporate more of it?

1.3 Planning the route, maps, and navigation

- What resources will you use to research your pilgrimage route?
- Have you booked accommodation and any places of interest or necessary aspects of the trip along the way?
- Are you confident that you will be able to navigate the route? If not, how can you gain that confidence?
- Which spots along the route do you want to spend more time in?
- Have you allowed time for serendipity?

1.4 Physical preparation and training

- What physical training and preparation will you undertake for your pilgrimage?
- What kinds of terrain and weather do you expect, and how can you replicate them in your training?
- Are you confident that you can get up and walk each day? If not, how will you gain this confidence?

1.5 What to take with you — and what to leave behind

- How will you stop yourself from taking too much stuff?
- Have you walked in your full gear as practice before leaving?
- How will you use your phone on pilgrimage?
- What emotional and spiritual baggage can you leave behind?

1.6 Preparing for the inner journey

- How will you prepare for the inner journey of pilgrimage before your departure?
- Will you set aside time each day for reflection during the pilgrimage? Do you plan to bring along a journal or another system for capturing your thoughts?
- What questions resonate with you?
- Can you add some of your own?

1.7 Facing fears

- What are you afraid of? Write down everything big and small, rational and irrational.
- How can you mitigate those fears?
- You can never get rid of all your fear. Is it worth going on pilgrimage anyway?

Part 2: The journey

2.1 The pilgrim's day

- How might the daily repetition of pilgrimage help you?
- Which parts of the pilgrim's day do you expect to find the most challenging?
- What brings you small moments of joy?

2.2 Walking in the path of history puts life in perspective

- What aspects of history form part of your pilgrimage route?
- Which are you interested in visiting?
- Sometimes it is the unexpected places that

mean the most. How can you keep an open mind so serendipity may alight at other times?

- How can 'memento mori' help you put life into perspective?

2.3 A glimpse of the divine in sacred places

- Where have you experienced this sense of the divine or felt that the veil is thin?
- How can you remain open to the spiritual aspects of pilgrimage without expectation of such moments?
- The end of a journey can be an important time for reflection. How will you mark the end of your pilgrimage?

2.4 Hardship as an element of pilgrimage

- If you are sick or suffering, how might pilgrimage help you?
- What might you have to adjust to ensure you can finish your pilgrimage?
- How do you cope with pain at the moment?

- How will you cope with pain as part of your pilgrimage?
- How can you prevent excessive pain?
- What will you do if the pain is too much?

2.5 Embrace the pilgrimage industry

- What are the pros and cons of the pilgrimage industry? How might it affect your pilgrimage?
- How can you embrace the industry — or avoid it completely?

2.6 Eating on pilgrimage

- What are your expectations of food on pilgrimage? How might it affect your trip positively or negatively?
- How can you leave behind some of your usual food-related behaviours and embrace the difference on your pilgrimage?
- Is there any essential food or drink you want to bring with you or determine the availability of along your route? Or are you happy to leave it to serendipity?

2.7 Facing the challenge

- Do you have starting energy? If not, how can you find it?
- Are you ready to commit to your pilgrimage?
- How will you develop pushing-through energy? Are there ways you can start practicing it in your daily life?
- If you are planning your pilgrimage, how can you make space for finishing energy on your return?

2.8 Pilgrimage in a changing season

- What season of your life are you in?
- What part might pilgrimage play in the transition between the seasons of life and your acceptance of it?

Part 3: Arriving and the return

3.1 Arriving on a pilgrimage

- What are your expectations of arriving on the final day of your pilgrimage? Can you release those expectations and just let it be whatever it is?

- How can you "allow time for your soul to catch up," as Phil Cousineau puts it?

3.2 Returning home

- How will you make time for your return to normal life?
- How will you reflect and learn from your experience?
- How can you allow time and space for the gifts of pilgrimage to emerge?

APPENDIX 2: PRACTICALITIES OF THE PILGRIMS' WAY

You can find my day-by-day breakdown of the route with pictures and more detail about each of the day's walk at:

www.booksandtravel.page/pilgrims-way

Distance: 180 kilometres (112 miles)

Books and resources:

Walking the Pilgrims' Way — Leigh Hatts

More information and downloadable GPX files for mapping: www.britishpilgrimage.org/portfolio/pilgrims-way-to-canterbury/

The Pilgrims' Way: Fact and Fiction of an Ancient Trackway — Derek Bright

Britain's Pilgrim Places — Nick Mayhew-Smith and Guy Hayward

British Museum's Thomas Becket exhibition website — www.britishmuseum.org/exhibitions/thomas-becket-murder-and-making-saint

Thomas Becket: Warrior, Priest, Rebel, Victim: A 900-Year-Old Story Retold — John Guy

Related fiction:

Tomb of Relics — J.F. Penn. A supernatural relic. A thousand-year-old conspiracy. A madman who turns death into art. I wrote this story after my pilgrimage about a relic of St Thomas Becket stolen from Canterbury Cathedral. www.jfpenn.com/book/tomb-of-relics/

The Crimson Thread — Anna Sayburn Lane. A theatrical curse. A murder in the cathedral. Only one woman can unravel the mystery and prevent more bloodshed.

I interviewed Anna about The History of England Written in Stone: Literary Canterbury here: www.booksandtravel.page/literary-canterbury/

Tour operators:

I booked this pilgrimage independently, but there are tour operators who do luggage transfer for some parts of the route.

www.responsibletravel.com/holidays/england-walking/travel-guide/the-pilgrims-way

www.walkawhile.co.uk

Accommodation:

Premier Inn, 135 Borough High St, London SE1 1NP. I always stay in Premier Inns if they are available. They are reasonably priced, in useful locations, and are safe and quiet. This one is near Southwark Cathedral and the start of the route.

I walked all the way out of London on the first day, but it was a big day's walk at over 40km, so you can choose to stop earlier and split the route.

Royal Victoria and Bull Hotel, 1 High St, Dartford DA1 1DU

Up the Downs B & B, 23 Northdown Rd, Kemsing, Sevenoaks TN15 6SD

Premier Inn (Allington), London Rd, Maidstone ME16 0HG. You can get a taxi to and from the route, which I did in the morning, as the roads are very busy. I only stayed in the Premier Inn as Aylesford Priory was closed because of the pandemic, but if you can stay there, then definitely do so. www.thefriars.org.uk

Dog & Bear Hotel, The Square, Lenham, Maidstone ME17 2PG

In Boughton Lees, I had booked online to stay at The Flying Horse, Wye Rd, Boughton Lees, Ashford TN25 4HH. But when I arrived that day, it was closed for the pandemic, so I stayed at the upmarket **Eastwell Manor**, Champneys Hotel & Spa, Eastwell Park, Ashford TN25 4HR which is close by. It was raining hard, and I didn't want to walk on, but the look on the face of the concierge was pretty funny as I walked in with my backpack, all wet and muddy, into the hotel lobby.

Canterbury Cathedral Lodge, The Precincts, Canterbury CT1 2EH. It is absolutely worth staying here if you can book in advance as you have access to the cathedral grounds after it's closed to the public.

More accommodation options for the route: www.thepilgrimsway.co.uk/bed-breakfast/

Facilities:

While the B & Bs on the route would have provided breakfast, I usually left too early. There are little shops and cafes as well as pubs along the way and you can usually eat after 6.30 p.m. in restaurants and pubs for dinner.

You can drink the tap water in the UK, so fill your water bottles at your accommodation.

APPENDIX 3: PRACTICALITIES OF THE ST CUTHBERT'S WAY

You can find my day-by-day breakdown of the route with pictures and more detail about each of the day's walk at:

www.booksandtravel.page/st-cuthberts-way-lindisfarne

Distance: 115 kilometres (71 miles)

Books and resources:

Walking St Oswald's Way and St Cuthbert's Way — Rudolf Abraham

More information and downloadable GPX files for mapping: www.britishpilgrimage.org/portfolio/st-cuthberts-way/

Britain's Pilgrim Places
— Nick Mayhew-Smith and Guy Hayward

St Cuthbert's Way: A Pilgrims' Companion
— Mary Low

To the Island of Tides: A Journey to Lindisfarne
— Alistair Moffat

Related fiction:

If you enjoy mysteries, I recommend the DCI Ryan books by L.J. Ross, which are all set in Northumberland. These include *Holy Island*, *Cuthbert's Way*, and more. www.ljrossauthor.com

I interviewed Louise about her favourite places in Northumberland here: www.booksandtravel.page/northumberland-lindisfarne-newcastle-ljross

You might also enjoy my modern-day thriller, *Day of the Vikings*, which is set partly on Lindisfarne: www.jfpenn.com/book/vikings/

You can get the ebook for free if you sign up at www.JFPenn.com/free

Tour operators:

I booked this pilgrimage independently, but there are tour operators if you prefer:

www.macsadventure.com/walking-holiday/uk-walking-holiday/scotland/st-cuthberts-way/

www.shepherdswalksholidays.co.uk/our-holidays/category/st-cuthbert-s-way

www.stcuthbertsway.info/services/tour-operators/

Before you book anything:

Plan your crossing to Lindisfarne and accommodation on the island before you book the rest, as this will determine where you stay the night before the crossing. There is limited accommodation around this area, so you need to book well in advance.

Tide times:
holyislandcrossingtimes.northumberland.gov.uk

Accommodation:

Premier Inn, Sandgate, Berwick-upon-Tweed TD15 1ER. (Berwick is pronounced Berrick). I always stay in Premier Inns if they are available. They are reasonably priced, in useful locations, and are safe and quiet.

I had the best fish stew of my life at The Queens Head a few doors down, which also has accom-

PILGRIMAGE

modation. 6 Sandgate, Berwick-upon-Tweed TD15 1EP

Station Hotel, 26 Market Square, Melrose TD6 9PT. I left early before breakfast and they gave me a packed lunch to take with me.

The Spread Eagle Hotel, 20 High St, Jedburgh TD8 6AG. There are plenty of shops and places to eat in Jedburgh and the Co-op opens early for supplies the next morning.

The Mill House B & B, Main St, Kirk Yetholm, Kelso TD5 8PE. They can provide a packed lunch as there are no shops between here and Wooler.

Noble Lands, High St, Wooler NE71 6BY. There is a Co-op supermarket to get supplies and a few restaurants and pubs in the town.

Fenham Farm, Beal, Berwick-upon-Tweed TD15 2PL. There is a shop at Fenwick to buy snacks, but it's best to order dinner at the farm in advance and they also have a lovely breakfast. This was one of the best B & Bs I've ever stayed in, and a beautiful location.

The Crown and Anchor, The Market Place, Fenkle St, Holy Island, Berwick-upon-Tweed TD15 2RX. Wonderful restaurant. Book well in advance.

Transport:

There are regular trains to Berwick-upon-Tweed from London north through Newcastle, or south from Edinburgh. Get the bus to Melrose from Berwick, Border Buses #60, or there is a direct bus from Edinburgh.

Get a taxi from Lindisfarne, Holy Island, back to Berwick-upon-Tweed. You can book one to come over when the tide goes out first thing.

Facilities:

Some days are walking across hills and in rural areas, and sometimes there weren't shops nearby, even at the end of the day. Check Google Maps around the accommodation you choose and take a packed lunch. You can usually eat after 6.30 p.m. in restaurants and pubs for dinner.

You can drink the tap water in the UK, so fill your water bottles at your accommodation.

APPENDIX 4: PRACTICALITIES OF THE CAMINO DE SANTIAGO PORTUGUESE ROUTE

You can find my day-by-day breakdown of the route with pictures and more detail about each of the day's walk at

www.booksandtravel.page/camino-portuguese-coastal-route/

Distance: 300 kilometres (186 miles)

Useful books:

There are many Camino guides for each route; I used *The Camino Portugués: A Wise Pilgrim Guide* as it was slender and light. I also cut out the pages I didn't need for my route to reduce the weight further.

A Pilgrim's Guide to the Camino Portugués — John Brierley, which has a more spiritual angle.

The Camino Portugués — Kat Davis

Pilgrim Tips & Packing List Camino de Santiago: What you need to know beforehand, what you need to take, and what you can leave at home — S. Yates with Daphne Hnatiuk. While I have offered as much practical advice as I can, this book provides lots more tips from experienced pilgrims who have done various Camino routes.

The Whole Sole Guide to Walking the Camino de Santiago: How I Walked Over 500 Miles Without Getting a Single Blister or Losing a Toenail — Maureen Sullivan

Related fiction:

The cathedral of Santiago de Compostela features in *Stone of Fire*, ARKANE #1, available for free on all ebook stores, as well as in print and audio.

www.jfpenn.com/book/stone-of-fire/

Pilgrimage podcast episodes:

I've discussed pilgrimage with several pilgrims on my Books and Travel podcast: www.booksandtravel.page/tag/pilgrimage/

I also recommend Sacred Steps with Kevin Donahue — www.sacredstepspodcast.com

Tour operators:

I booked with MacsAdventure.com and they organised the accommodation and provided an excellent app, which included water and toilet stops as well as the route.

www.macsadventure.com/camino-tours/

They used local operator www.tee-travel.com

Other pilgrims I met along the way recommended www.caminoways.com

Accommodation:

Hotel Sandeman, Largo Miguel Bombarda Nº3, Vila Nova de Gaia, Porto, Portugal. I stayed a few nights here exploring Porto before starting the Camino.

Hotel PortoBay Teatro, Rúa de Sa de Bandeira, Porto, Portugal

Hotel Axis Vermar, Rúa da Imprensa Regional, Póvoa de Varzim, Portugal

Hotel Suave Mar, Av. Engenheiro Arantes de

Oliveira, Esposende, Portugal

Hotel Laranjeira, Rúa Candido dos Reis, Viana do Castelo, Portugal

Hotel Meira, Rúa 5 de Outubro, 56, Vila Praia de Ancora, Portugal

Hotel Vila da Guarda, Calle Tomiño, 8 - Calle Pontevedra, Spain

Casa Puertas, Rúa Vicente López, 7 - Arrabal, Oia, Spain

Hotel Pazo de Mendoza, Plaza Pedro de Castro, Baiona, Spain

Sercotel Hotel Bahía Vigo, Rúa Cánovas del Castillo, 24, Vigo, Spain

Hotel Isape, Carretera de Soutomaior, 36, Arcade, Spain

Hotel Rías Bajas, Rúa Daniel de la Sota, 7, Pontevedra, Spain

Hotel Pousada Real, Rúa Real, 58, Caldas de Reis, Spain

A Casa Antiga do Monte, Boca do Monte-Lestrove, Padrón - Dodro, Spain (This was several kilometres outside of Padrón off the Camino, so I would not choose to book this myself)

Hotel Costa Vella, Rúa da Porta da Pena, 17, 15704 Santiago de Compostela, Spain. I booked two nights here privately. They have a lovely garden and it's a short walk to the cathedral and centre of town.

You can get a taxi or public transport to the airport (SCQ) which is only about twenty minutes from the centre.

Facilities:

All my accommodation included breakfast, and it was my main meal of the day. I usually bought some food the day before to carry with me, but often there were cafes and small supermarkets along the route.

Portuguese restaurants are usually open from 12.00 noon until around 4.00 p.m. for lunch, then close until 8.00 p.m. when they open again for dinner. This was usually too late for me, so I often just bought something from a supermarket for early evening, and ate a bigger breakfast.

You can drink the tap water in Portugal and Spain, so I filled up my water bottles from the tap every day rather than buying water.

There are plenty of toilets along the way, although I did stop a few times in forests and woods when necessary.

APPENDIX 5: GEAR AND KIT LIST

Every trip requires an assessment of the terrain and the expected weather conditions, as well as a decision on whether you will carry your own pack.

I carried my pack on each of the three pilgrimages, and I certainly made the mistake of carrying too much gear, especially on the St Cuthbert's Way.

This is my kit list for the Camino, by which time I had learned the lesson of carrying too much.

Backpack

I carried all my gear and used an Osprey Sirrus 36 with an in-built pack cover for the rain. I was really happy with the size and weight of the pack. I didn't get any hip bruising as I did on the St Cuthbert's Way, and I didn't get any back or shoulder pain either. It weighed about 8kgs and I also carried water, so it was about 9.5kg in total each day.

Small bag

With all my gear in my backpack, I also carried a Tom Bihn Cubelet, which is just a simple pouch. Inside were my phone (for photos and app for directions), my passport and pilgrim's Credential for stamps, lip salve, antihistamine tablets, euros in coins, and a few notes for coffee, plus a whistle in case of emergency.

Hiking shoes

Keen Walking Shoes — waterproof. I was going to wear summer hiking shoes, but I checked the weather forecast and knew I'd be doing some full rain days, so I went with my autumn shoes.

Walking poles

LEKI Women's Micro Vario Carbon Trekking Poles. These are really light and they also fold into three pieces so I could fit them in my pack for the flight over and return. You can't take walking poles in hand-luggage, but they are non-negotiable in my opinion, especially if you carry your own pack. I used them almost every day on the uneven ground, in the rain, and also for steadying tired legs.

Water bottles

I carried a 1 litre and a 0.75 litre bottle, but some days I didn't drink it all. There are fountains and shops on the way so you can refill. You can drink the tap water in Portugal and Spain, so I just refilled from taps and fountains.

Walking clothes

I wore the same thing every day and washed everything in the shower on arrival every day, then hung it to dry. North Face quick-drying T-shirt (or any kind of sport top), North Face quick-dry walking trousers with zips that turn them into shorts, 2 x pairs of socks, thin and thick, hat and sunglasses, neck buff (which I prefer to sun cream on my neck but isn't necessary if you use a wider brim hat).

Other things:

Clothes and underwear for the evening post-arrival and shower. I had another pair of trousers, a wraparound sarong, and another T-shirt and a linen long-sleeved shirt for the sun as well as underwear.

Long-sleeved warm top for layering. I didn't take a jumper, as the weather forecast was good enough not to need one.

Waterproof jacket. Jack Wolfskin summer waterproof. I didn't take waterproof over-trousers as I am happy to walk in normal walking trousers or shorts as they are quick dry. Some pilgrims take ponchos, but they are useless in the wind as they flap around so much. A normal waterproof jacket + pack cover is enough (for my route and weather conditions anyway).

Sandals or flip-flops for the evening and I also wore these on my days off in Porto and Santiago de Compostela

First aid kit. I needed blister plasters, normal plasters in a roll + small scissors, painkillers (ibuprofen and paracetamol), needle and thread. I had to buy some antiseptic spray and top up my stock of plasters and painkillers, but there were pharmacies in every town that were open late, so that was never a problem.

Dry bag x 2. I put my clothes inside a bigger dry bag in my pack, and I have a mini dry bag for my phone, passport, and Credential which fit into the Tom Bihn bag.

Zip-top bags for sundries. I carried minimal toiletries in several zip-top bags. Travel hairbrush, tiny sample size bottle of hair oil instead of conditioner (all accommodations had soap and shampoo), small sun cream, small moisturiser, prescription medication, toothbrush + tiny toothpaste, deodorant, spork (spoon and fork combo which I used for yoghurt and other things in the evenings as I tended to buy supermarket food rather than go to restaurants).

Eye mask and ear plugs. Critical for a good night's sleep!

Journal + pen, and a guidebook for the Camino, which I used in addition to the app. Even though the route is way-marked, you need some kind of guide or map, so you know where to go if you find yourself walking alone. I also took my Kindle to read on.

Multi-plug European adaptor, external battery for my phone, which I used on several long days, headphones, and charging cables

Shoulder tote bag for days in the city and also supermarket shopping

Several other **plastic bags** — useful for carrying food for the day or keeping wet things away from other stuff

Face mask or face covering — needed for pharmacies and also the plane flights as when I traveled; Spain still had some COVID rules

What I carried and didn't need:

Swimming costume — If you love to swim, then there are plenty of places to do so on the Portuguese coastal route, as well as some hotels with pools. But I was usually too tired to want to swim and as I walked alone, I couldn't leave my pack on the beach in the middle of the day. So I didn't use my costume, but I'd probably still recommend taking one if you are so inclined.

Mini travel umbrella — I was grateful for my umbrella in Porto as it rained a LOT, but then I carried it all the way to Santiago de Compostela. On the worst rainy days walking, I just used my raincoat anyway, so I should have left it in Porto.

Mini coffee flask — I definitely run on coffee, especially in the mornings, and there were frequently no cafes open if I left early for the day's walk. I used the flask a couple of times, but not as much as I expected, so I could have done without it.

Adjust your gear by season and terrain

I definitely carried too much in my pack for both the Pilgrims' Way and the St Cuthbert's Way, but these were the things that I needed for the different season, terrain, and weather conditions.

Warm layers — Beanie hat + neck scarf, long-sleeved warm top, fleece jumper, extra socks, trainers for the evening

Waterproofs — Stronger waterproof jacket, waterproof trousers, waterproof gloves (which I was grateful for on freezing cold days in the rain), waterproof socks (useful for crossing the sands to Lindisfarne). I also had a bright poncho, reflective yellow bands, and a head torch for walking in the dusk or the rain.

APPENDIX 6: SELECTED BIBLIOGRAPHY

Practical guides:

A Pilgrim's Guide to the Camino Portugués
— John Brierley

Britain's Pilgrim Places
— Nick Mayhew-Smith and Guy Hayward

Pilgrim Tips & Packing List Camino de Santiago: What you need to know beforehand, what you need to take, and what you can leave at home
— S. Yates with Daphne Hnatiuk

Walking the Pilgrim's Way — Leigh Hatts

Walking St Oswald's Way and St Cuthbert's Way
— Rudolf Abraham

The Camino Portugués: A Wise Pilgrim Guide — Michael Matynka Iglesias

The Whole Sole Guide to Walking the Camino de Santiago: How I Walked Over 500 Miles Without Getting a Single Blister or Losing a Toenail — Maureen Sullivan

Mindset:

Alone Time: Four Seasons, Four Cities, and the Pleasures of Solitude — Stephanie Rosenbloom

A Philosophy of Walking — Frédéric Gros

In Praise of Walking: The new science of how we walk and why it's good for us — Shane O'Mara

Pilgrimage: Journeys of Meaning — Peter Stanford

The Art of Pilgrimage: The Seeker's Guide to Making Travel Sacred — Phil Cousineau

Walking: One Step at a Time — Erling Kagge

We Are Pilgrims: Journeys in Search of Ourselves — Victoria Preston

Wintering: The Power of Rest and Retreat in Difficult Times — Katherine May

Finding meaning in midlife:

Life Reimagined: The Science, Art, and Opportunity of Midlife — Barbara Bradley Hagerty

Menopausing: The Positive Roadmap to Your Second Spring — Davina McCall

The Salt Path — Raynor Winn

ACKNOWLEDGEMENTS

Thanks to Jonathan for supporting my solo wandering, for looking after me when I was sick, and for always encouraging me.

Thanks to Dan Clarke, my personal trainer, for helping me prepare for the walks, and for keeping my writing life pain-free.

Thanks to my readers, as well as my listeners and patrons at The Creative Penn Podcast and Books and Travel. I hope this book helps some of you take the next step.

Thanks to Kristen Tate at The Blue Garret for editing and encouragement.

Thanks as ever to Jane Dixon Smith, JD Smith Design, for cover design and print interior formatting.

www.JFPenn.com

www.ingramcontent.com/pod-product-compliance
Lightning Source LLC
Chambersburg PA
CBHW072048110526
44590CB00018B/3087